Light Manufacturing in Tanzania

DIRECTIONS IN DEVELOPMENT
Private Sector Development

Light Manufacturing in Tanzania

A Reform Agenda for Job Creation and Prosperity

Hinh T. Dinh and Célestin Monga
with contributions by Jacques Morisset, Josaphat Kweka,
Fahrettin Yagci, and Yutaka Yoshino

THE WORLD BANK
Washington, D.C.

Contents

Boxes

Figures

Tables

Foreword

The list of countries that have achieved the highest rates of economic growth in the world over the past 20 years is puzzling. It includes the usual suspects, such as China and India, but also a growing number of African countries. Tanzania is one of them. Yet, few people know that the East African country once considered one of the most rigid experiments in socialism now ranks among the global top performers. Growth has been driven to a large extent by the boom in telecommunications, financial services, and construction. However, structural transformation has been limited, and the contribution of manufacturing to gross domestic product remains lower today than it was in 1970.

Lessons of history and economic policy show that Tanzania's remarkable growth performance cannot be sustained without structural transformation that benefits all workers. The main question is whether Tanzania's growth model is sufficiently inclusive to generate enough decent jobs to meet the needs of the country's young and often unskilled workforce, which is still employed mostly in traditional agriculture and informal activities.

The question on the minds of policy makers at the highest levels of government is how exactly to achieve such a goal. Fortunately, Tanzania is a country of abundance, with significant development resources and big dreams. It is richly endowed with minerals and gas. It has a great geographic location, and its people are hardworking and entrepreneurial. It also has a stable polity with well-tested democratic institutions. Tanzania's long-term vision is to become a middle-income country that is characterized by high-quality livelihoods, peace, stability, unity, good governance, a well-educated and learning society, and a strong and competitive economy.

Light Manufacturing in Tanzania makes the case that, if Tanzania is to remain one of the most rapidly growing economies in Sub-Saharan Africa, it has to make progress in the structural transformation that can lift workers from low-productivity agriculture and the informal sector to high-productivity activities. Manufacturing, which has been the main vehicle throughout the world to achieve this transformation, has been stunted in Tanzania even though some progress has been observed in recent years, notably through the development of regional markets. This book shows that feasible, low-cost, sharply focused policy initiatives aimed at enhancing private investment could launch Tanzania on a path to competitive light manufacturing.

Light Manufacturing in Tanzania has several innovative features. First, it provides in-depth cost comparisons between Tanzania and four other countries in Africa and Asia at the sectoral and product levels. Second, the book relies on a wide array of quantitative and qualitative techniques to identify the key constraints on enterprises and to evaluate differences in the performance of firms across countries. Third, it uses a focused approach to identify country- and industry-specific constraints. Fourth, it highlights the interconnectedness of constraints and solutions. For example, solving the manufacturing input problem requires actions in agriculture, education, and infrastructure.

Detailed cross-country analysis has been carried out on four light manufacturing sectors in Tanzania: textiles and apparel, leather and leather products, wood and wood products, and agroprocessing. Based on this analysis, *Light Manufacturing in Tanzania* suggests that government policies should be directed toward removing the constraints in a few of the most promising light manufacturing sectors using practical and innovative solutions inspired by the rapidly growing Asian economies that started from a point 20 years ago that was not so different from the starting point of Tanzania today.

Philippe Dongier
Country Director for Burundi, Tanzania, and Uganda
Africa Region
The World Bank

Acknowledgments

This book has been prepared by a team composed of Hinh T. Dinh (Lead Economist and Team Leader), Célestin Monga (Senior Advisor), Jacques Morisset (Lead Economist), Josaphat Kweka (Senior Economist), Fahrettin Yagci (Consultant), and Yutaka Yoshino (Senior Economist). It is part of a larger World Bank project on Light Manufacturing in Africa conducted by a core team consisting of Hinh T. Dinh (Team Leader), Vincent Palmade (Co-Team Leader), Vandana Chandra, Frances Cossar, Tugba Gurcanlar, Ali Zafar, Eleonora Mavroeidi, Kathleen Fitzgerald, and Gabriela Calderon Motta. The Tanzania book has benefited from valuable comments by Andrea Mario Dall'Olio (Lead Economist and Private Sector Development Leader), David Rosenblatt (Economic Advisor and Peer Reviewer), Volker Treichel (Lead Economist and Peer Reviewer), and Paolo Zacchia (Lead Economist). The work has been carried out with the support and guidance of the following senior managers of the World Bank: Justin Yifu Lin (former Senior Vice President and Chief Economist), Oby Ezekwesili (former Vice President, Africa Region), Kaushik Basu (Senior Vice President and Chief Economist), Makhtar Diop (Vice President, Africa Region), Philippe Dongier (Country Director for Burundi, Tanzania, and Uganda), Mercy Miyang Tembon (Country Manager), Shanta Devarajan (Chief Economist, Africa Region), Zia Qureshi (Director, Operations and Strategy Department, Development Economics), Gaiv Tata (Director, Africa Finance and Private Sector Development), and Marilou Uy (Senior Advisor, Special Envoy Office and Former Director, Africa Finance and Private Sector Development). We thank the following Bank staff for their unfailing encouragement and support: Alphonsus J. Marcelis, Geremie Sawadogo, Dipankar Megh Bhanot, Aban Daruwala, Saida Doumbia Gall, Nancy Lim, and Melanie Brah Marie Melindji.

The team has benefited from the support of the Tanzanian government, particularly Benno Ndulu (Governor, Bank of Tanzania), Philip Mpango (Executive Secretary, Planning Commission, Office of the President of Tanzania), and Paul Maduka Kessy (Deputy Executive Secretary, Planning Commission, Office of the President of Tanzania). The team has also received key inputs from the following in Washington, DC: Global Development Solutions, LLC of Reston, Virginia, under the direction of Yasuo Konishi, Glen Surabian, and David Phillips; Dan Kasirye (Africa Region, International Finance Corporation); and Yan Wang and Jian Zhang (World Bank); and the following in Tanzania: Eline

Sikazwe (Director, Industry), Consolatha Ishebabi (Director, Small and Medium Enterprise Development), Edward Sungula (Director, Policy and Planning), Elli Pallangyo (Assistant Director, Investment and Industrial Development), Elias Ernest (Principal Trade Officer), and Mizuno Yoshino (Industrial Advisor, Japanese Technical Assistance) of the Ministry of Industry and Trade; Mike Laiser (Director General, Small Industries Development Organization); Emmanuel Kalenzi (Resident Representative, United Nations Industrial Development Organization); Hussein Kamote (Director of Policy and Advocacy, Confederation of Tanzanian Industries); Joram P. Wakari (Executive Secretary, Leather Association of Tanzania); Adam Zuku (Senior Chamber Development Officer, Chamber of Commerce, Industry, and Agriculture); Peter Lanya (Vice Chairman, Tanzania Exporters Association); Adelhelm Meru (Director General) and Lameck Borega (Investors Facilitation Officer) of the Export Processing Zone Authority; Edwin Rutegaruki (Director, Domestic Market Development) and Samuel Mvingira (Director, Research and Planning) of the Tanzania Trade Development Authority; Pankaj Kumar (Chief Operating Officer, ALAF Limited); Nassoro Balasa (General Manager, Tanzania-China Friendship Textile/ Urafiki); Hillary Miller-Wise (Country Director, TechnoServe Tanzania); Justin Stokes (Senior Competitiveness Advisor, Tanzania Private Sector Foundation); Wilfred Mbowe (Principal Economist), David Kwimbele (Principal Economist), Peter Stanslaus (Economist), Obadia Kiwelu (Economist), and Geoffrey Mwambe (Economist) of the Bank of Tanzania; Peter Njau (Assistant Director, Veterinary Services, Ministry of Livestock and Fisheries Development); and the field research assistance of George Gandye (Consultant) and Michael Ndanshau (Consultant).

The report has been edited by a team headed by Robert Zimmermann and Meta deCoquereaumont. The team also thanks Paola Scalabrin and Kristen Iovino for production support of the book. The financial support of the Bank-Netherlands Partnership Program and the Japan Policy and Human Resources Development Fund is gratefully acknowledged.

About the Authors

Hinh T. Dinh is Lead Economist in the Office of the Senior Vice President and Chief Economist of the World Bank. Previously, he served as Lead Economist in the Africa Region (1998–2008), the Finance Complex (1991–98), and the Middle East Region at the Bank (1979–91). He received his undergraduate degrees with high honors in economics and mathematics from the State University of New York and his MA in economics, MS in industrial engineering, and PhD in economics from the University of Pittsburgh. His research focuses on public finance, international finance, industrialization, and economic development. His latest books include *Light Manufacturing in Africa* (2012), *Performance of Manufacturing Firms in Africa* (2012), *Light Manufacturing in Zambia* (2013), and *Tales from the Development Frontier* (2013).

Célestin Monga is Senior Advisor at the World Bank. He is also the Director of the forthcoming Oxford University Press *Handbook of Africa and Economics*. He was the Economics Editor of the five-volume *New Encyclopedia of Africa* (2007). He has served on the Board of Directors of the Sloan School of Management's Fellows Program at the Massachusetts Institute of Technology and taught economics at Boston University and the University of Bordeaux (France). Prior to joining the World Bank, he was Department Head and Manager in the Banque Nationale de Paris group. His books are translated into several languages. He holds degrees from the Massachusetts Institute of Technology, Harvard, and the universities of Paris 1 Panthéon-Sorbonne, Bordeaux, and Pau.

About the Contributors

Josaphat Kweka is Senior Economist in the Poverty Reduction and Economic Management unit of the World Bank, where he has been managing analytical and advisory work, including in trade and regional integration, special economic zones, enterprise development, and the tourism industry. Before joining the Bank in 2007, he was a Senior Research Fellow at the Economic and Social Research Foundation (Dar es Salaam), where he worked for 10 years on several policy research studies and was Director of the Globalization Project. He received his undergraduate and master's degrees in economics from the University of Dar-es-Salaam and PhD in economics from the University of Nottingham, the United Kingdom.

Jacques Morisset is the World Bank Lead Economist in Tanzania. After earning his PhD in economics from the University of Geneva, he has held various positions in the World Bank and International Finance Corporation, while collaborating with the World Economic Forum. He has published in academic journals, including the *World Bank Economic Review, Journal of Development Economics,* and *World Development.* He has been a member of the Board of the *World Bank Economic Review.*

Fahrettin Yagci is a World Bank retiree currently teaching economics at Bosphorus University, Istanbul. He worked in Asia, Europe, the Middle East, and 20 countries in Africa during his 22 years of service at the Bank. His areas of responsibility included trade policy, industrial policy, agriculture, and macroeconomics. Before joining the Bank, he taught economics at several universities in Ankara and Istanbul and also worked for the Turkish government. He received his PhD in economics from the London School of Economics.

Yutaka Yoshino is a Senior Economist in the Africa Region at the World Bank. He received a bachelor of laws from Sophia University in Tokyo, master of international affairs from Columbia University, and MA and PhD in economics from the University of Virginia. Prior to the World Bank, he was an Economic Attaché at the Permanent Mission of Japan to the United Nations. His research interests include the domestic investment climate and economic integration in low-income economies; economic geography and regional integration; South-South trade and investment; and trade, the environment, and natural resources.

Abbreviations

AGOA	African Growth and Opportunity Act (United States)
CR	concentration ratio
DRC	domestic resource cost
EPZ	export processing zone
EPZA	Export Processing Zones Authority
EU	European Union
FDI	foreign direct investment
f.o.b.	free on board
FYDP	Five Year Development Plan
GDP	gross domestic product
IIDS	Integrated Industrial Development Strategy 2025
ISIC	International Standard Industrial Classification
NACTE	National Council for Technical Education
RCA	revealed comparative advantage
SEZ	special economic zone
SIDO	Small Industries Development Organization
SME	small and medium enterprise
VETA	Vocational Education and Training Authority

Note: All dollar amounts are U.S. dollars ($) unless otherwise indicated.

Overall Context

The chapters in part 1 provide the overall context of light manufacturing in Tanzania. Chapter 1 presents the rationale for the study, the potential of the sector in creating jobs and prosperity for Africa, and the approach and methodology of the study. Chapter 2 reviews Tanzania's recent economic performance and prospects and concludes that, despite good macroeconomic performance, the country still needs to pursue structural transformation and diversification. Moreover, despite Tanzania's abundant natural endowments, manufacturing remains a viable source for job creation and prosperity. Chapter 3 examines the overall business environment among firms of all sizes in light industry in Tanzania. It first reviews the macroeconomic framework, focusing on wages, exchange rates, and interest rates before analyzing the microeconomic issues affecting firms such as export incentives, trade logistics, and access to electricity, land, and finance. Competition, an issue of paramount importance in improving Tanzania's competitiveness, is analyzed next, before a discussion of a potential shortcut for addressing some of the related macro and micro problems.

CHAPTER 1

A Good Potential in Light Manufacturing

This analysis of the potential of light manufacturing in Tanzania, part of a larger project covering China, Ethiopia, Tanzania, Vietnam, and Zambia, draws on several analytical tools:

- World Bank Enterprise Surveys[1]
- Qualitative interviews with about 300 enterprises (both formal and informal, of all sizes) in all five countries[2]
- Quantitative interviews with representatives of some 1,400 enterprises (of all sizes, both formal and informal) in all five countries[3]
- In-depth interviews with about 300 formal medium enterprises that were focused on the value chain in all five countries[4]
- A study of the impact of Kaizen managerial training among owners of small and medium enterprises (SMEs); this training, delivered to about 250 entrepreneurs in Ethiopia, Tanzania, and Vietnam, was led by Japanese researchers from the Foundation for Advanced Studies on International Development and the National Graduate Institute for Policy Studies (World Bank 2011)

For a detailed discussion of why we have chosen these five countries and the particular analytical tools, see Dinh and others (2012).[5]

This publication discusses practical ways to increase the competitiveness of specific manufacturing sectors that could have positive impacts on job creation and prosperity. In contrast with most studies of Africa's growth potential, which repeatedly yield long lists of general constraints (including infrastructure, education, corruption, and red tape), our study identifies a smaller number of more specific key constraints that vary by sector and firm size. Narrowing the list of constraints can make the reform agenda more manageable given the limited financial and human resources in most African countries, including Tanzania.

The report presents an in-depth diagnosis of the constraints in four light manufacturing sectors in Tanzania that we have identified for their good growth potential: textiles and apparel, leather and leather products, wood and wood products, and agroprocessing.

We have identified six main constraints across sectors and firms that impede the competitiveness of light manufacturing in Tanzania: the availability, cost, and quality of inputs; access to industrial land; access to finance; entrepreneurial capabilities, both technical and managerial; worker skills; and trade logistics. Among small firms, the most important constraints are in entrepreneurial skills, land, inputs, and finance. Among large firms, the most important constraints are associated with trade logistics, land, and inputs.

We propose policy reforms to address the constraints in Tanzania based on successes in other countries. Because binding constraints vary by country, sector, and firm size, policy makers need to accomplish the following:

- Have a clear idea of the most promising manufacturing sectors and then identify, prioritize, and remove the most serious constraints in these sectors.
- Keep targeted policies selective, consistent with comparative advantage, and in line with a country's resources and capacity.
- Use conventional policies and nonconventional policies, such as plug-and-play industrial zones.
- Start small and build gradually; success breeds success.

Why Light Manufacturing?

Light manufacturing (including agribusiness) is labor intensive and allows low-income countries to compete by leveraging their low labor costs. It has been a crucial stepping-stone for most successful developing economies, including China, Mauritius, Vietnam, and the East Asian tigers. Developing light industry also permits countries to earn foreign exchange, create jobs, raise wages for the vast pools of underemployed labor, and build new technical and managerial skills. African countries would likewise have the opportunity to leverage competitive or potentially competitive input industries—in, for example, agricultural products, leather, and wood—to help advance the competitiveness of the light manufacturing industries.

Manufacturing has long been recognized as an engine of growth. In industrial countries, economic growth has always been associated with indigenous manufacturing capability. Nicholas Kaldor's first law of economic growth states that "the faster the rate of growth of the manufacturing sector, the faster will be the rate of growth of … [gross domestic product (GDP)] … for fundamental economic reasons connected with induced productivity growth inside and outside the manufacturing sector" (Thirlwall 1983, 345). In a study on advanced countries, Kuznets (1959) notes that modern economic development is punctuated by long periods of rapid output growth that coincide with a structural shift in the composition of output away from agriculture

and into manufacturing. Even in wealthy countries where the share of manufacturing in output and employment has been stagnant or declining, there is
evidence that, relative to nonmanufacturing sectors, manufacturing involves
more production links with other sectors and the transfer of more production
skills.

Most African countries have identified potential sources of growth through
Poverty Reduction Strategy Papers or equivalent documents. However, the
sectors have generally been selected without a cohesive methodology. This
chapter argues that, for countries that have chosen a systematic focus on
manufacturing as a development strategy, there is a clear case for governments,
cooperating closely with the private sector, to pay particular attention to the light
manufacturing sectors, including agribusiness, in which their countries could
compete. The private sector should lead in the identification of products, while
the government plays a supporting role.

Identifying Opportunities in Light Manufacturing

For existing products, revealed comparative advantage (RCA) and the domestic
resource cost (DRC) can be used to pinpoint industries in which increased
production could accelerate industrialization (box 1.1). We have calculated
the DRC for each product on which we have a value chain analysis, and we have
identified the relevant constraints and the measures to remove these
constraints.

For new products, latent comparative advantage, identified using the
growth identification and facilitation framework, can pinpoint industries
that are likely to be consistent with a country's comparative advantage
(Lin and Monga 2011). The framework postulates that, while a country's
endowments, including its infrastructure, are given at a specific time and
determine its comparative advantage, endowments change over time in a
rapidly growing country. Thus, the comparative advantage of a successful
country is dynamic (Grossman and Helpman 1991; Krugman 1987; Lin and
Chang 2009). Some of a successful country's dynamically growing industries
will lose their comparative advantage as the economy's endowment structure upgrades. These sunset industries will then become the sunrise industries of countries that have lower income levels and less capital-intensive
endowments, and that will therefore have a latent comparative advantage
in the industries.

The Potential for Light Manufacturing in Africa

For most Sub-Saharan African countries, light manufacturing is an attractive
choice in the effort to capitalize on human and natural resource endowments
and generate more employment and more well paying jobs for the many
low-skilled laborers in the informal sector. While the technological complexity of

Box 1.1 Calculating the RCA and the DRC

The revealed comparative advantage (RCA)—also called the Balassa index, after Balassa (1965)—is an index that shows the relative advantage or disadvantage of a country in exporting a commodity as indicated by actual export patterns relative to those of all other countries in the world. It is defined as follows:

$$RCA = (E_{ij}/E_{iw})/(E_{wj}/E_{wn}) \qquad (B1.1.1)$$

where E_{ij} refers to exports of commodity j by country i; w is the set of countries; and n is the set of all commodities. A country has a revealed comparative advantage in commodity j if the RCA is greater than 1 and a comparative disadvantage in commodity j if the RCA is less than 1.

While the RCA is an indirect measurement of comparative advantage based on trade patterns that are actually revealed and observed in the trade data, the domestic resource cost (DRC) directly measures a country's comparative advantage in an industry based on factor prices, the foundation of comparative advantage. For an import-dependent country, the DRC is particularly valuable in determining whether a government ought to foster exports that generate foreign exchange or whether it ought instead to support import replacement that conserves foreign exchange. The DRC, widely used as an index of economic efficiency in restrictive trade regimes, is defined by Bruno (1972) as follows:

$$d_j = \frac{-\sum_{s=2}^{m} \overline{f_{sj}} v_s}{u_j - m_j} \qquad (B1.1.2)$$

where d_j is the DRC of product j; m is the number of primary factors; n is the number of products; v_s is the accounting (shadow) price for the sth primary factor ($s = 1$ is the foreign exchange); f_{sj} is the difference between the marginal dollar revenue of commodity j (u_j) and the (marginal) dollar import requirements for the unit production of commodity j (m_j), and a *bar* represents the total (direct and indirect) primary factors of production.

A DRC of less than 1 indicates that the cost of the domestic resources needed to produce a unit of the good is less than the potential foreign exchange earnings from exporting the product; that is, the country has a comparative advantage in the product, and there is a rationale for the government to foster growth in manufacturing and exporting the product. A DRC greater than 1 indicates that the cost of the domestic resources to produce the good for the domestic market is more than the foreign exchange required to import the good; that is, the country does not have a comparative advantage in the good, and the government should not be supporting import-substitution policies with respect to the good. The DRC and RCA are calculated based on the current and prevailing conditions, which reflect existing resource endowments and policies. Policy reforms could change the DRC value over time. For industries that pass the DRC test, whether for exports or import substitution, integrated value chain studies can map the constraints to policy recommendations and identify what the government should do to promote the expansion of the identified industries.

many manufacturing industries may have increased since the East Asian tigers emerged, several labor-intensive industries, such as apparel, footwear, and furniture, still need unskilled workers.[6] Millions of low-skilled informal workers in East Asian and some South Asian countries have been lifted out of poverty through the growth of light manufacturing. For example, in Fujian and Guangdong provinces in China, the industrial labor force swelled from 6 million in 1985 to 11 million at the end of 2001 (likely an understatement, given the large number of migrant workers) (Naughton 2007). Official data indicate that 83 million Chinese were employed in the manufacturing sector in 2002 (NBS 2003).

Beyond its capacity to stimulate job creation, the strong connection between light manufacturing and trade also supports the development choice to focus on light manufacturing. The case for export-led growth is well established for developing countries (Chenery 1980; Commission on Growth and Development 2008; Harrison and Rodríguez-Clare 2010). Harrison and Rodríguez-Clare (2010) find that export-oriented countries have grown more rapidly, though establishing causality is difficult. Trade also enables developing countries to take advantage of the important learning that is derived from exposure to global competition and then to import the skills and technology necessary to move up the value chain.

Tanzania and many other African countries have the necessary inputs for a competitive light manufacturing sector: a comparative advantage in low-wage labor, abundant natural resources sufficient to offset the lower labor productivity compared with their Asian competitors, privileged access to high-income markets for exports, and a sufficiently large local or regional market to allow emerging producers to develop capabilities in quick-response, high-volume production and quality control in preparation for the breakthrough into highly competitive export markets.

These countries can follow the course pioneered by a succession of Asian countries by accelerating the realization of latent comparative advantage in segments of light manufacturing in which specific, feasible, sharply focused, low-cost policy interventions can deliver a quick boost to output, productivity, and perhaps exports, opening the door to expanded entry and growth.

Growing Markets Inside and Outside Africa

In recent years, four factors have been especially influential in opening new markets for Africa's light manufacturing firms:

- More rapid economic growth, accompanied by accelerating urbanization, has expanded the domestic market for manufactures in most countries. These new (urban) markets are offering fresh opportunities, including in Tanzania (especially Dar es Salaam, which is viewed as the ninth most rapidly growing city in the world).
- Foreign investors and bilateral aid agencies are investing in the production of manufactures destined for their own markets or other foreign markets.

Examples include the U.S. Agency for International Development's technical assistance to Tanzanian farmers.

- For globally competitive light manufacturing firms in Sub-Saharan Africa, the market is the world. In 2005, the United States established new trade preferences under the African Growth and Opportunity Act (AGOA), granting products from low-income African countries extraordinarily favorable access to the U.S. market; the European Union (EU) did the same under the Cotonou Agreement and the Everything But Arms Initiative. These trade preferences are critical to the success of African exporters in the global apparel market (for example, because, without the preferences, African exporters in these markets are not competitive with more efficient global exporters) (World Bank 2010).[7]

- Regional integration, by increasing the size of regional markets, raises the attractiveness of these markets. The deepening regional integration arrangements in which Tanzania participates, particularly the initiative to establish a common market within the East African Community, are opening new markets for the country's exporters.

China's Growing Labor Cost Disadvantage: An Opportunity for Africa

Chinese products have penetrated almost every corner of the globe. In 2004, China supplied 18 percent of the combined value of all imports in the U.S. and European Union markets; by 2008, its share had nearly doubled, to 35 percent. To export light manufacturing products successfully, Sub-Saharan African producers will have to compete with China.

But the capacity of firms in the coastal provinces of China to outperform their rivals in low-income countries in price and quality in the global markets for labor-intensive light industry manufactures is declining inexorably. Growing numbers of coastal export firms in China are facing the prospect of being priced out of global markets for an expanding array of labor-intensive light industrial products as the labor market absorbs China's large pool of low-skilled workers and labor costs rise rapidly. Some of the displaced production will shift to China's inland provinces, but new manufacturing clusters are already appearing in Bangladesh and Cambodia, for example, where labor is cheap, though the infrastructure and supply chain arrangements cannot match the desirable conditions available in coastal areas of China such as Dongguan and Shenzhen.

Rising wages, stricter enforcement of labor and environmental regulations, the gradual expansion of costly safety net provisions, and the likely increase in the international value of the yuan mean that China's comparative advantage in exports of labor-intensive manufactures will continue to be eroded, perhaps at an even more rapid rate. China's efforts to limit the upward drift of its currency have contributed to domestic inflation, which is spurring wage demands and accelerating the narrowing of cost advantages in labor-intensive manufactures.

This is creating an opening for other low-wage producers if they can learn to compete. For Sub-Saharan African countries, this represents an opportunity to jump-start structural changes that hold the promise of delivering large, sustained increases in output, exports, employment, productivity, and incomes. However, low-income countries in East Asia, South Asia, and the Middle East and North Africa will be energetic contenders for the newly available slices of the global market. The challenge facing Sub-Saharan African firms is to find ways to compete with firms in Bangladesh, Cambodia, the Lao People's Democratic Republic, and Nepal, which have low wages and large pools of low-skilled workers. But even a small slice of an enormous global market would create millions of higher-productivity and higher-wage jobs in Sub-Saharan Africa.

Resolve the Critical Constraints in Promising Sectors

Despite favorable observations on the macroeconomy and the business environment in Sub-Saharan Africa, there are multiple obstacles to accelerating development and structural transformation, particularly in finance, infrastructure (electricity, roads), governance, and human capital. However, unlike past policy prescriptions, which appeared too daunting to achieve, we have identified constraints that are both more specific and more readily resolved.

Past Policy Prescriptions: Intimidating To-Do Lists

Studies of the constraints on the expansion of light manufacturing in Sub-Saharan Africa have usually involved staggeringly long lists that suggest no feasible set of policy adjustments would lead to a result attractive to investors. Often, the implication has been that, unless all the shortcomings are fixed, the sector could not grow.

Yet, developing economies in other regions have expanded production and exports of light manufactures without first resolving the sorts of constraints observed in Sub-Saharan Africa. China in the mid-1970s and early 1980s suffered from low product quality (sewing machines that leaked oil onto fabric, electric motors that failed in hot, humid weather), passive management (a manager at a large plant insisted that he did not know the unit cost of his product; another, asked to explain the presence of numerous idle workers, said, "If we don't employ them, where would they go?"), administrative confusion (would-be investors that abandoned the Xiamen special economic zone after managers failed to provide set prices for land, electricity, and water), delays in moving merchandise through customs and port facilities, and indifference to customer needs (Dinh and others 2013).

Emerging manufacturers in Sub-Saharan Africa must, of course, compete with today's Chinese firms, not with the much weaker Chinese firms of the 1980s. However, powerful market forces have begun to undermine the competitive advantage of China's well-established coastal centers of labor-intensive manufacturing. As the profits of these producers of apparel, leather products, and other labor-intensive manufactures are squeezed, the firms will either shift to other lines of business or move to the interior, to other Asian countries, or, as suggested in this book, to African countries such as Tanzania and Zambia.

A More Feasible Approach

We use the results of our intensive study of four light industry sectors to identify concrete packages of specific, feasible, and inexpensive policy initiatives that can maximize Tanzania's opportunity to jump-start its growth in production, employment, and exports. We have selected these four sectors as representative examples of labor-intensive light manufacturing industries that have a history of production in developing economies. The analysis of specific value chains is therefore only representative of a larger group of industries in which Tanzania may find it has an advantage. Focusing on specific industries highlights the constraints that exist and provides valuable information on which we may base targeted recommendations.

Our recommendations draw on the experience of countries such as China and Vietnam, which have built thriving light industries despite difficult initial conditions. While it will be challenging for African manufacturers to match the price and quality advantages of the well-established market leaders in China's coastal regions, the gradual erosion of the competitive advantage of Chinese firms will create more opportunities for African companies to expand domestic sales of labor-intensive manufactures. Later, with the accumulation of experience and financial strength, African firms can enter regional and global markets in competition with new entrants from China's interior and from countries such as Bangladesh and Cambodia, which suffer from some of the same constraints as the African economies.

The approach we follow relies on five separate sources of data and methodology, including the value chain analysis, to identify the binding constraints in each sector. We are thus able to trim the list to a few leading constraints. Setting such a priority has made the exercise more manageable, the policy actions more precise, and the sequencing more appropriate. The approach builds on the work of Hausmann, Rodrik, and Velasco (2005), who visualize development as a continuous process of specifying the binding constraints that limit growth, formulating and implementing policies to relax the constraints, securing modest improvements in performance, and then renewing growth by identifying and pushing against the factors limiting expansion in the new environment. It is also consistent with the new structural economics approach, which views economic development as a process that requires the continuous introduction of new and better technologies in existing industries and the upgrading of labor- and resource-intensive industries to new, more capital-intensive industries (Lin 2010).

Following Hausmann, Rodrik, and Velasco (2005), our approach emphasizes that development begins somewhere, but not everywhere. In Africa, as in China, applying limited funding and administrative personnel to implement a set of sharply focused reforms holds the promise of initiating new clusters of production, employment, and, eventually, exports without first resolving econ-omy-wide problems of land acquisition, utility services, skill shortages, adminis-trative shortcomings, and the like.

Notes

1. See Enterprise Surveys (database), International Finance Corporation and World Bank, Washington, DC, http://www.enterprisesurveys.org.
2. The questionnaire was developed by John Sutton of the London School of Economics and Political Science.
3. The interviews were conducted by the Centre for the Study of African Economies at Oxford University, based on a questionnaire designed by Marcel Fafchamps and Simon Quinn of Oxford University.
4. The interviews were conducted by Global Development Solutions (see GDS 2011).
5. For details, see "Light Manufacturing in Africa: Targeted Policies to Enhance Private Investment and Create Jobs," Data and Research, World Bank, Washington, DC, http://go.worldbank.org/ASG0J44350.
6. Panagariya (2008, 286) argues that "greater expansion of unskilled–labor-intensive sectors still offers greater scope for the employment of unskilled labor .... No evidence is available showing that shifts in technologies have narrowed the relative differences between unskilled-labor intensities across sectors. As for the magnitude of expansion, the world markets offer huge scope for it. If policies are right, India could replace China as the manufacturing hub of unskilled–labor-intensive products of the world."
7. The recent severe contraction in apparel production in Madagascar after the removal of the country's AGOA eligibility is a case in point.

References

Balassa, Bela. 1965. "Trade Liberalization and 'Revealed' Comparative Advantage." *Manchester School of Economic and Social Studies* 33 (2): 92–123.

Bruno, Michael B. 1972. "Domestic Resource Costs and Effective Protection: Clarifications and Synthesis." *Journal of Political Economy* 80 (1): 16–33.

Chenery, Hollis B. 1980. "Interactions between Industrialization and Exports." *American Economic Review* 70 (2): 281–87.

Commission on Growth and Development. 2008. *The Growth Report: Strategies for Sustained Growth and Inclusive Development.* Washington, DC: World Bank. https://openknowledge.worldbank.org/handle/10986/6507.

Dinh, Hinh T., Vincent Palmade, Vandana Chandra, and Frances Cossar. 2012. *Light Manufacturing in Africa: Targeted Policies to Enhance Private Investment and Create Jobs.* Washington, DC: World Bank. http://go.worldbank.org/ASG0J44350.

Dinh, Hinh T., Thomas G. Rawski, Ali Zafar, Lihong Wang, and Eleonora Mavroeidi. 2013. *Tales from the Development Frontier: How China and Other Countries Harness Light Manufacturing to Create Jobs and Prosperity.* With contributions from Tong Xin and Pengfei Li. Washington, DC: World Bank.

GDS (Global Development Solutions). 2011. *The Value Chain and Feasibility Analysis; Domestic Resource Cost Analysis.* Vol. 2 of *Light Manufacturing in Africa: Targeted*

Policies to Enhance Private Investment and Create Jobs. Washington, DC: World Bank. http://go.worldbank.org/6G2A3TFI20.

Grossman, Gene M., and Elhanan Helpman. 1991. *Innovation and Growth in the Global Economy.* Cambridge, MA: MIT Press.

Harrison, Ann E., and Andrés Rodríguez-Clare. 2010. "Trade, Foreign Investment, and Industrial Policy for Developing Countries." In *The Handbook of Development Economics*, edited by Dani Rodrik and Mark R. Rosenzweig, 4039–4214. *Handbooks in Economics*, Vol. 5. Amsterdam: Elsevier North Holland.

Hausmann, Ricardo, Dani Rodrik, and Andrés Velasco. 2005. "Growth Diagnostics." John F. Kennedy School of Government, Harvard University, Cambridge, MA.

Krugman, Paul R. 1987. "The Narrow Moving Band, the Dutch Disease, and the Competitive Consequences of Mrs. Thatcher: Notes on Trade in the Presence of Dynamic Scale Economies." *Journal of Development Economics* 27 (1–2): 41–55.

Kuznets, Simon. 1959. *Six Lectures on Economic Growth.* Glencoe, IL: The Free Press.

Lin, Justin Yifu. 2010. "New Structural Economics: A Framework for Rethinking Development." Policy Research Working Paper 5197, World Bank, Washington, DC.

Lin, Justin Yifu, and Ha-Joon Chang. 2009. "DPR Debate: Should Industrial Policy in Developing Countries Conform to Comparative Advantage or Defy It? A Debate between Justin Lin and Ha-Joon Chang." *Development Policy Review* 27 (5): 483–502.

Lin, Justin Yifu, and Célestin Monga. 2011. "Growth Identification and Facilitation: The Role of the State in the Dynamics of Structural Change." *Development Policy Review* 29 (3): 259–310.

Naughton, Barry J. 2007. *The Chinese Economy: Transitions and Growth.* Cambridge, MA: MIT Press.

NBS (China, National Bureau of Statistics). 2003. *China Labor Statistical Yearbook 2003.* Beijing: China Statistics Press.

Panagariya, Arvind. 2008. *India: The Emerging Giant.* London: Oxford University Press.

Thirlwall, A. P. 1983. "A Plain Man's Guide to Kaldor's Growth Laws." *Journal of Post Keynesian Economics* 5 (3): 345–58.

World Bank. 2010. *Investing across Borders 2010: Indicators of Foreign Direct Investment Regulation in 87 Economies.* Washington, DC: Investment Climate Advisory Services, World Bank.

———. 2011. *Kaizen for Managerial Skills Improvement in Small and Medium Enterprises: An Impact Evaluation Study.* Vol. 4 of *Light Manufacturing in Africa: Targeted Policies to Enhance Private Investment and Create Jobs.* Washington, DC: World Bank. http://go.worldbank.org/4Y1QF5FIB0.

CHAPTER 2

A Country with Great Potential

Tanzania is a low-income country and has the prospect of meeting only half the Millennium Development Goals despite high economic growth rates (6.1 percent a year since 1996) (Chuhan-Pole and Angwafo 2011). The share of the population living below the basic-needs poverty line declined by only 5.5 percentage points between 1990 and 2008 (from 39.0 to 33.5 percent). Tanzania's gross national income per capita in 2010 was $500, less than half the average in Sub-Saharan Africa ($1,125). Economic growth has been driven by mining, construction, communications, and the financial sector; manufacturing, transport, and tourism have also played a role.

The limited impact of economic growth on poverty alleviation is partly rooted in the slow structural transformation observed in Tanzania over the past decade, perhaps reflecting the absence of targeted interventions in sectors that have the highest potential for employment and growth. In fact, the share of manufacturing declined from 13 percent of gross domestic product (GDP) in the 1970s to around 10 percent in 2010 (MOF 2010). More than 70 percent of the labor force still works in traditional agriculture. At less than 10 percent of GDP, manufacturing's role in the economy is marginal. Its share in the country's exports was well below 20 percent from 1995 to 2010, which is less than half the 40 percent share reported in most industrialized middle-income countries. While manufacturing exports have expanded considerably since 2005 (from a low base), the sector as a whole must grow two more times as quickly over the next 15 years relative to the 6.6 percent average over the last 15 years if the country is to transition to middle-income status by 2025 (Moyo and others 2012).

Tanzania is achieving good but unequal progress in primary, secondary, and tertiary school enrollments, which will give the country the strong knowledge base needed to support industrialization. However, only 3 percent of the workforce is classified as highly skilled, and 13 percent is classified as medium skilled (figure 2.1). In many middle-income countries, the corresponding rates are around 12 and 33 percent, respectively (Moyo and others 2012).

About two-thirds of the country's population is under age 24 and underemployed, including people with college and university degrees. Creating jobs for

Figure 2.1 The Distribution of Labor Force Skills, Tanzania and Middle-Income Countries

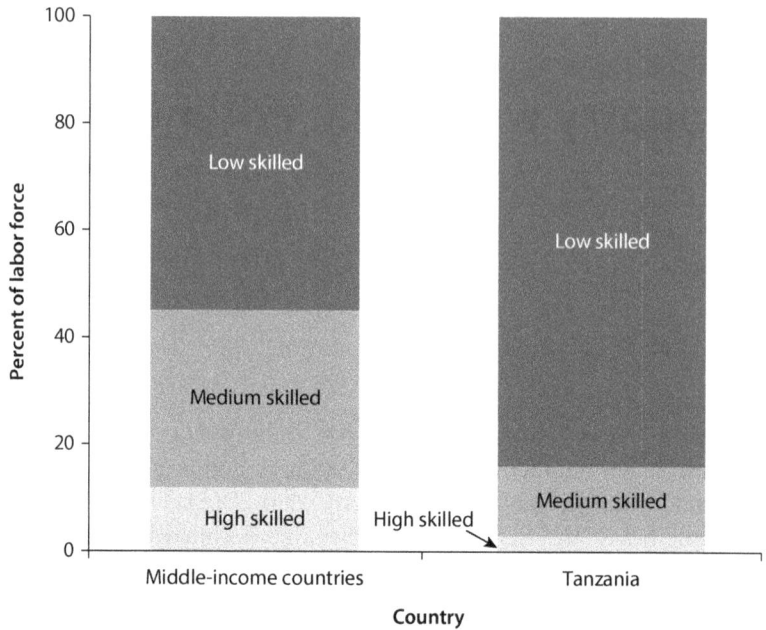

Source: Moyo and others 2012.

this growing population of young people is a key challenge. Urban unemployment rates are as high as 30 percent, especially among youth with little schooling. The number of underemployed workers is even higher, as people cannot afford not to work in a poor country such as Tanzania. The share of formal employment (that is, employment benefiting from formal social protection) is less than 10 percent of the workforce. Many workers are obliged to cumulate jobs. The average wage is around $45 in urban areas, barely above the subsistence level.

Good Macroeconomic Performance, but Limited Structural Transformation

Over the past 15 years, Tanzania has transitioned from a centralized to a market economy and dramatically improved its economic performance (table 2.1). The government introduced a series of comprehensive economic reforms. These began with partial liberalization, which was followed by a push for far-reaching structural reforms. Since 1996, major reforms have included the introduction of fiscal and monetary policies to control inflation, fiscal consolidation, stronger public financial management, the privatization or reform of state-owned enterprises, and a pullback in state interventions in the economy through trade reform, liberalization of the financial sector, and creation of a market-oriented regulatory framework.

Table 2.1 Selected Macroeconomic Indicators, Tanzania, 1990–2010

Percent

Indicator	1990	2000	2005	2008	2009	2010
GDP growth	7.0	4.9	7.4	7.4	6.0	7.0
Growth in gross national income	—	5.1	7.2	7.4	6.0	7.3
Gross capital formation, share of GDP	26.0	17.0	23.0	27.0	30.0	31.0
Gross domestic savings, share of GDP	10.0	13.0	17.0	13.0	21.0	20.0
Adjusted net savings, share of GDP	10.0	12.4	8.5	3.2	10.7	11.7

Source: World Development Indicators (database), World Bank, Washington, DC, http://data.worldbank.org/data-catalog/world-development-indicators.
Note: — = not available, GDP = gross domestic product.

Figure 2.2 Annual GDP Growth, Tanzania

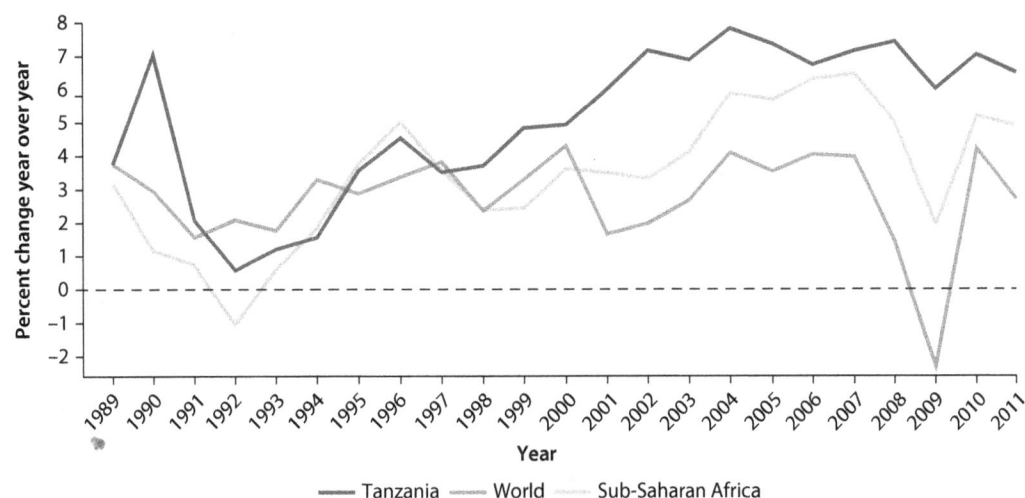

Source: World Development Indicators (database), World Bank, Washington, DC, http://data.worldbank.org/data-catalog/world-development-indicators.

The sound macroeconomic framework has also attracted a large volume of foreign aid, helping the government expand the fiscal envelope. While this has contributed to growth in government consumption and expenditure, overall investment, particularly private investment, is not substantial. Past economic growth in Tanzania was also clearly not synchronized with private investment, unlike the situation in countries such as China and Thailand. While Tanzania has seen an increase in private investment in recent years, partly because of growth in the financial sector, the size of private investment is still limited relative to other countries when they were at a similar level of GDP per capita as Tanzania today.

Beginning in the mid-1990s, inflation declined to single digits, and economic growth improved. The liberalization of trade and of the exchange rate regime boosted nontraditional exports and reversed the growing external imbalances. GDP growth averaged 5 percent a year over 1990–2010 (figure 2.2).

Although agriculture is Tanzania's largest economic sector, employing some 75 percent of the workforce, the performance there has been disappointing because productivity has stagnated over the past three decades, which is in sharp contrast with successful agricultural countries such as Thailand and Vietnam.[1] Manufacturing output dropped and has only recently risen, and tourism has emerged as an important sector, contributing more than 10 percent to GDP. Mining is also growing as the result of massive foreign investment in the gold sector.

Macroeconomic stabilization and structural reforms have been instrumental in attracting foreign direct investment (FDI), a key factor in fostering greater nonagricultural growth. The fiscal incentives for foreign investors have been instrumental as well. A mining act that provides generous fiscal arrangements for investors was adopted in 1998, inviting a surge in foreign investment in the mining sector, especially gold mining, during the following decade. FDI rose from $282 million in 2000 to $700 million in 2010, or 2 percent of GDP (UNCTAD 2011). Donors supported the government's reforms through large inflows of official donor assistance. Macroeconomic management is sound, and the country's risk of debt distress is moderate. Reflecting growing confidence among domestic consumers and investors, gross national savings rose from around 13 percent of GDP in 2000 to 20 percent in 2010.

Despite these positive signs, the country seems to be stuck in a dual economy stage, lagging in structural transformation and industrialization and lacking the necessary infrastructure and human capacity to accelerate broad-based growth. The positive medium-term outlook for an average growth of 8 percent will depend on timely investments to tackle bottlenecks in infrastructure and labor productivity and to implement structural reforms (especially to improve the business climate), as well as prudent fiscal and monetary policies (Yoshino 2012).

The main question is whether Tanzania's growth model will yield enough good jobs to meet the needs of its young, educated workforce. The basic structure of the economy, as measured by sectoral contributions to GDP, has changed little in the past 40 years (figure 2.3). The share of manufacturing in GDP shrank from 13 percent in the 1970s to 9.8 percent in 2010, though a rebound has been observed recently. Agricultural productivity has stagnated, and agricultural value added has grown at only about 4 percent a year since 2000, but merely 1 percent in per capita terms. However, even that growth has been driven mainly by expansions in the amount of land under cultivation rather than by boosting productivity (World Bank and Ministry of Planning 2007). Once a leading exporter of traditional agricultural products, Tanzania now lags behind many newcomer agricultural exporters. Raw materials make up nearly 60 percent of its exports (MOF 2011).

The absence of structural transformation is especially evident in the labor market. Economic growth in recent years has taken place in capital- and skill-intensive sectors, but has created few jobs. Traditional agriculture still employs

Figure 2.3 Indicators of Structural Transformation, Tanzania, 1970–2010

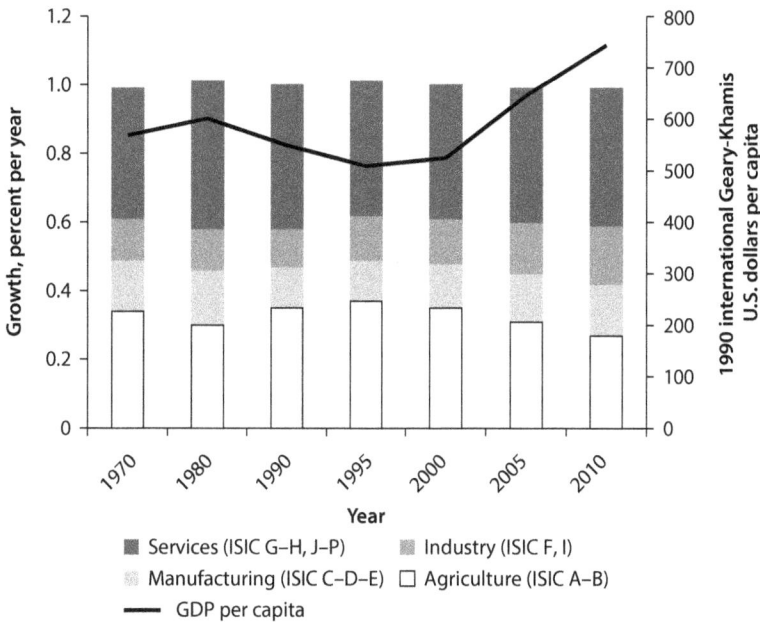

Sources: Maddison n.d.; World Development Indicators (database), World Bank, Washington, DC, http://data.
worldbank.org/data-catalog/world-development-indicators.
Note: ISIC = International Standard Industrial Classification of All Economic Activities. For the significance of
the ISIC codes, see "Detailed Structure and Explanatory Notes: ISIC Rev.4," Statistics Division, Department of
Economic and Social Affairs, United Nations, New York, http://unstats.un.org/unsd/cr/registry/regcst.
asp?Cl=27.

most of the workforce. Only 5 percent of new entrants to the labor market work
in the formal and modern sectors. The household enterprise sector is Tanzania's
most rapidly growing source of employment. Integrated Labor Force Survey data
show that employment in household enterprises grew 13 percent over 2000–06,
greater than the change in the overall labor force and greater than the rate of
growth in wage employment in both the nonagricultural and the agricultural
sectors (figure 2.4). Employment has grown too slowly to absorb the influx of
young and educated workers, particularly in urban areas.

Clearly, despite good macroeconomic performance, Tanzania still needs to
pursue structural transformation and diversification. Tanzania's growth pattern
also needs to be more pro-poor so that consumption grows more quickly among
lower-income segments of the population. Tanzania's growth incidence curve,
which shows how widely income and consumption growth are shared across the
population, slopes upward, indicating that poorer households have shared less in
growth relative to richer households (figure 2.5). In contrast, Uganda's curve
slopes downward, indicating that consumption has grown more rapidly among
poorer households relative to richer households.

Figure 2.4 Growth in Employment, by Primary Sectors, Tanzania, 2000–06

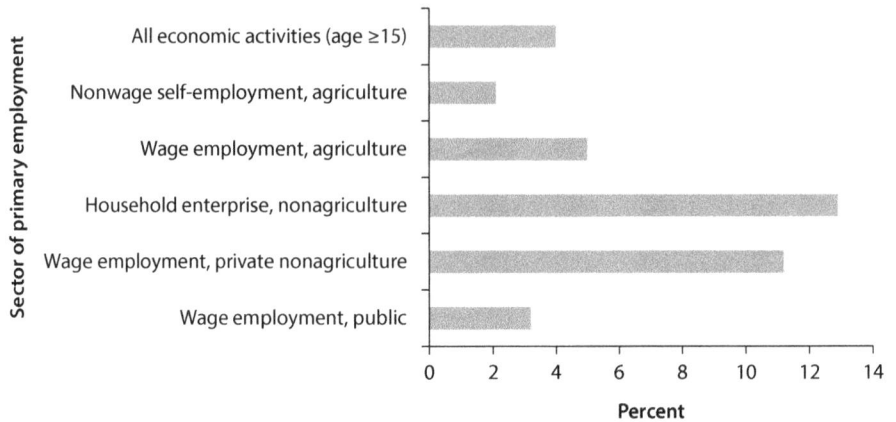

Source: NBS and Ministry of Planning 2007.

Figure 2.5 Growth Incidence Curves, Ghana, Mozambique, Tanzania, and Uganda

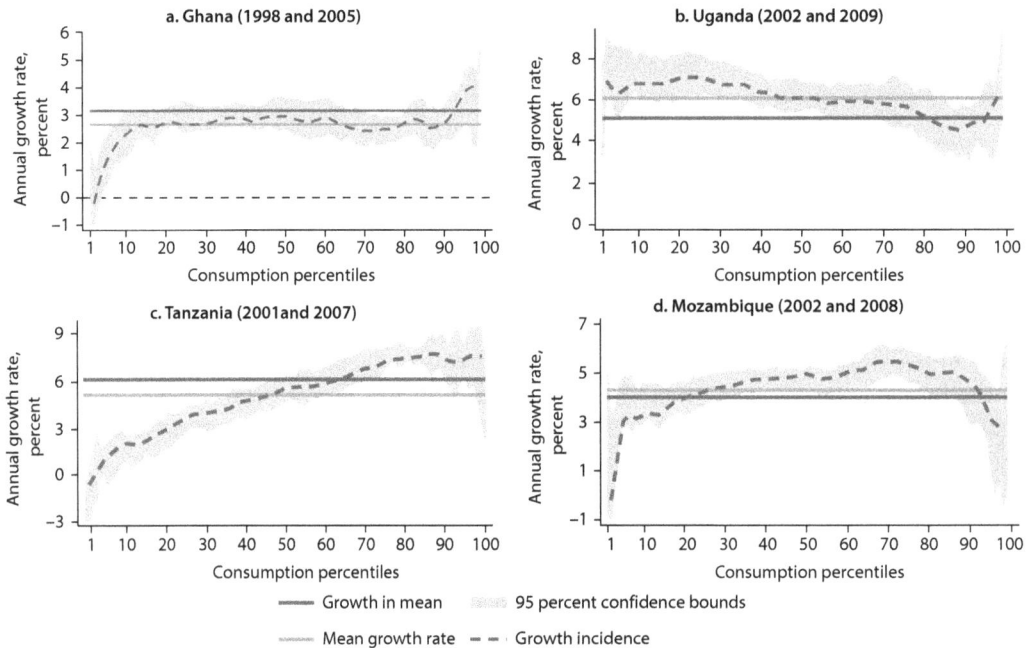

Source: IMF 2011.

Seizing the Moment: Opportunities for Tanzania

A growth strategy for Tanzania should be based on the country's two main comparative advantages. The first is the country's natural endowments, including agricultural land, minerals, natural gas, and access to global markets through its ports. These endowments offer unique opportunities to create links with manufacturing activities by providing cheap and diversified inputs and customer markets, which are both necessary for the emergence of a competitive industrial sector. The second comparative advantage is the country's low-cost labor relative to Asian countries.

Tanzania is richly endowed with natural gas and minerals, including gold, diamonds, gemstones, coal, iron, uranium, nickel, chrome, tin, and platinum. Coal, uranium, and industrial minerals such as soda, kaolin, tin, gypsum, phosphate, and dimension stones are mined at competitive economic costs. Commercial production of natural gas began on Songo-Songo Island in the Indian Ocean in 2004. The gas is piped to Dar es Salaam, where most of it is converted to electricity by public and private operators. Following major gas discoveries in Tanzania's offshore deepwater regions, the country's proven natural gas reserves have risen from 7.5 trillion to approximately 30.0 trillion cubic feet.

However, developing these minerals, while bringing foreign exchange resources to the country, creates few jobs and, in fact, can generate problems because of the volatility of the related revenues and governance, given the weak institutional-industry links (Sayeh 2012). Indeed, the most serious problem arising from the development of natural resources is that few jobs are created, especially the productive jobs needed in economies where unemployment or severe underemployment is high. Furthermore, pressures on the real exchange rate (the Dutch Disease) tend to discourage labor-intensive growth in other sectors in a resource-based economy. The increase in natural resource revenues boosts national income and demand, inducing a shift in production from the tradable sector to the nontradable sector and appreciation in the real exchange rate as a result of the higher prices of nontraded goods relative to traded goods (Corden 1984; Corden and Neary 1982). This raises the costs of inputs in the rest of the economy, particularly in the exporting sectors. Because the mineral sector uses fewer inputs and is less dependent on domestically produced goods, sectors such as manufacturing and agriculture lose their profitability and competitiveness against imports. Ultimately, the nonmineral export sector contracts; the public sector expands; and inflation rises. The adverse impact of resource wealth on the tradable sectors is commonly associated with low economic growth. This is why few developing countries have managed to benefit greatly from their natural resources and why those that have benefited are still struggling with unemployment. This provides an additional reason why policies to facilitate the growth of manufacturing are even more important in a resource-based economy relative to a non–resource-based economy.

Thus, economic performance in Tanzania is at a turning point. The economy has been growing rapidly for 15 years, but experience elsewhere shows that growth cannot be sustained without a structural transformation that shifts workers from low-productivity agriculture and the informal sector to higher-productivity activities. Tanzania has yet to undergo this transformation. Labor-intensive light manufacturing has led in the structural transformation of the most successful economies, and it can do the same in Tanzania.

The remainder of this book addresses in detail the binding constraints on light manufacturing in Tanzania.

Note

1. For workforce data, see World Development Indicators (database), World Bank, Washington, DC, http://data.worldbank.org/data-catalog/world-development -indicators.

References

Chuhan-Pole, Punam, and Manka Angwafo. 2011. *Yes Africa Can: Success Stories from a Dynamic Continent*. Washington, DC: World Bank.

Corden, W. Max. 1984. "Booming Sector and Dutch Disease Economics: Survey and Consolidation." *Oxford Economics Paper* 36 (3): 359–80.

Corden, W. Max, and J. Peter Neary. 1982. "Booming Sector and Deindustrialization in a Small Open Economy." *Economic Journal* 92 (368): 825–48.

IMF (International Monetary Fund). 2011. *Regional Economic Outlook, Sub-Saharan Africa: Recovery and New Risks*. World Economic and Financial Surveys (April). Washington, DC: IMF.

Maddison, Angus. n.d. "Historical Statistics of the World Economy: 1–2008 AD." Excel document, Groningen Growth and Development Center, University of Groningen, Groningen, Netherlands. http://www.ggdc.net/maddison/Historical_ Statistics/horizontal-file_02-2010.xls.

MOF (Tanzania, Ministry of Finance and Economic Affairs). 2010. *The Economic Survey 2009*. Dar es Salaam, Tanzania: MOF.

———. 2011. *The Economic Survey 2011*. Dar es Salaam, Tanzania: President's Office and Planning Commission.

Moyo, Mujobu, Rebecca Simson, Arun Jacob, and François-Xavier de Mevius. 2012. "Attaining Middle Income Status; Tanzania: Growth and Structural Transformation Required to Reach Middle-Income Status by 2025." Working Paper 11/1019 (January), International Growth Centre, London. http://www.theigc.org/sites/default/ files/attaining_middle_income_status_in_tanzania.pdf.

NBS (Tanzania, National Bureau of Statistics) and Ministry of Planning, Economy, and Empowerment. 2007. "Integrated Labor Force Survey 2006." NBS, Dar es Salaam, Tanzania.

Sayeh, Antoinette M. 2012. "Opening Remarks." Paper presented at the Democratic Republic of Congo and the International Monetary Fund "Conference on the Management of Natural Resources in Sub-Saharan Africa," Kinshasa, Democratic Republic of Congo, March 21–22. http://www.imf.org/external/np/seminars/ eng/2012/kinshasa/pdf/as.pdf.

UNCTAD (United Nations Conference on Trade and Development). 2011. *Trade and Development Report, 2011: Post-crisis Policy Challenges in the World Economy*. Geneva, Switzerland: UNCTAD.

World Bank and Tanzania, Ministry of Planning, Economy, and Empowerment. 2007. *Main Report*. Report 39021-TZ. *Vol. 1* of *Tanzania: Sustaining and Sharing Economic Growth*. Country Economic Memorandum and Poverty Assessment. Washington, DC: Poverty Reduction and Economic Management Unit, Africa Region, World Bank. https://openknowledge.worldbank.org/handle/10986/7703.

Yoshino, Yutaka. 2012. *Tanzania, Tanzania Poverty Reduction Support Credit 9: P112762; Implementation Status Results Report: Sequence 01.* World Bank, Washington, DC. http://documents.worldbank.org/curated/en/2012/12/17133339/tanzania-tanzania -poverty-reduction-support-credit-9-p112762-implementation-status-results-report- sequence-01.

CHAPTER 3

The Business Environment

This chapter examines the overall business environment among firms of all sizes in light industry in Tanzania. It surveys, first, the macroeconomic framework, including wages, exchange rates, and interest rates; second, the microeconomic issues affecting firms, such as export incentives, trade logistics, and access to electricity, land, and finance; third, the concentration of firms in industries in Tanzania, competition policy, and the effect of trade policy and domestic regulations on competition; and, fourth, a potential shortcut for addressing some of the related macro and micro problems: plug-and-play industrial parks.

The Macroeconomic Framework

Wages (adjusted for productivity), exchange rates, and interest rates are critical macroeconomic variables affecting trade competitiveness. This section compares the level and evolution of these variables in several light industry sectors in China and in Tanzania.[1]

Nominal wages are lower in Tanzania than in China (table 3.1), but labor productivity in the two countries is similar in this sample (except in apparel) (table 3.2).[2] This gives Tanzania a production cost advantage in most sectors because of the lower labor costs in that country (wages adjusted for productivity); apparel, where Tanzania has a 2 percent labor cost disadvantage, is an exception. However, the costs of other inputs and of trade logistics are higher in Tanzania than in China. These cost disadvantages more than offset the labor cost advantage and result in higher total production costs in Tanzania relative to China in a number of sectors, with the notable exception of leather products in this sample.

Manufacturing wages are higher in Tanzania than in the other African countries except Zambia, and firms also have to pay a 6 percent skill development levy (a payroll tax) in Tanzania, which is high relative to international averages of 1–3 percent. Our interview respondents reported that the private sector does not benefit much from this tax because firms still have to train their employees; one-third of the revenues from the levy finance the Vocational Education and Training Authority.[3] The tax raises costs and impedes international competitiveness.

Table 3.1 Monthly Wages in Light Manufacturing, by Skill Level, Five Countries
U.S. dollars

Product	China		Vietnam		Ethiopia		Tanzania		Zambia	
	Skilled	Unskilled	Skilled	Unskilled	Skilled	Unskilled	Skilled	Unskilled	Skilled	Unskilled
Polo shirts	311–370	237–296	119–181	78–130	37–185	26–48	107–213	93–173	n.a.	n.a.
Dairy milk	177–206	118–133	—	31–78	30–63	13–41	150–300	50–80	106–340	54–181
Wooden chairs	383–442	206–251	181–259	85–135	81–119	37–52	150–200	75–125	200–265	100–160
Crown corks	265–369	192–265	168–233	117–142	181–	89–	—	—	–510	–342
Leather loafers	296–562	237–488	119–140	78–93	41–96	16–33	160–200	80–140	—	—
Milled wheat	398–442	192–236	181–363	78–207	89–141	26–52	200–250	100–133	320–340	131–149
Average	305–399	197–278	154–235	78–131	77–131	35–53	153–233	80–130	284–364	157–208

Source: GDS 2011.

Note: The upper values for crown corks (bottle caps) are not available for Ethiopia. The lower values for crown corks are not available for Zambia. n.a. = not applicable; — = not available.

Table 3.2 Labor Productivity in Light Manufacturing Sectors, Five Countries

Sector	China	Vietnam	Ethiopia	Tanzania	Zambia
Polo shirts, pieces per employee per day	18–35	8–14	7–19	5–20	n.a.
Leather loafers, pieces per employee per day	3–7	1–6	1–7	4–6	—
Wooden chairs, pieces per employee per day	3.0–6.0	1.0–3.0	0.2–0.4	0.3–0.7	0.2–0.6
Crown corks, pieces per employee per day × 1,000	13–25	25–27	10	—	201[a]
Wheat processing,[b] tons per employee per day	0.2–0.4	0.6–0.8	0.6–1.9	1.0–22.0	0.6–1.6
Dairy farming, liters per employee per day	23–51	2–4	18–71	10–100	19–179

Source: GDS 2011.
Note: n.a. = not applicable; — = not available.
a. Production is fully automated.
b. Data are from a sample of small enterprises in all five countries.

Figure 3.1 Changes in the Real Effective Exchange Rate, Chinese Yuan and Tanzanian Shilling, 2000–10

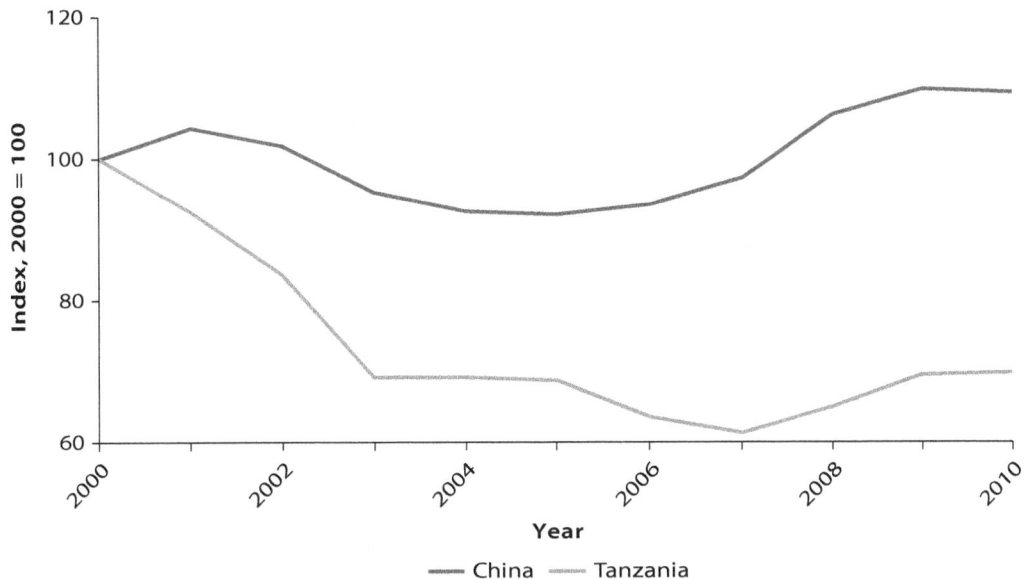

Sources: Based on data in International Financial Statistics (database), International Monetary Fund, Washington, DC, http://elibrary-data.imf.org/FindDataReports.aspx?d=33061&e=169393; and World Economic Outlook Database, International Monetary Fund, Washington, DC, http://www.imf.org/external/pubs/ft/weo/2011/02/weodata/index.aspx.

The exchange rate, a key macroeconomic price, is also crucial to competitiveness. An appreciating exchange rate reduces competitiveness by reducing exports and stimulating imports. A depreciation has the opposite effect. A comparison of the evolution of the real effective exchange rate for the Chinese yuan and the Tanzanian shilling shows that, after a slight appreciation in 2001, the Chinese yuan depreciated until 2005 and then appreciated again before stabilizing in 2009 (figure 3.1).[4] The real effective exchange rate of the Tanzanian shilling depreciated until 2007 and then appreciated until 2009. By and large, the real effective exchange rate in Tanzania depreciated relative to the Chinese yuan, as we should expect.

Figure 3.2 Real Lending Rates, China and Tanzania, 2000–10

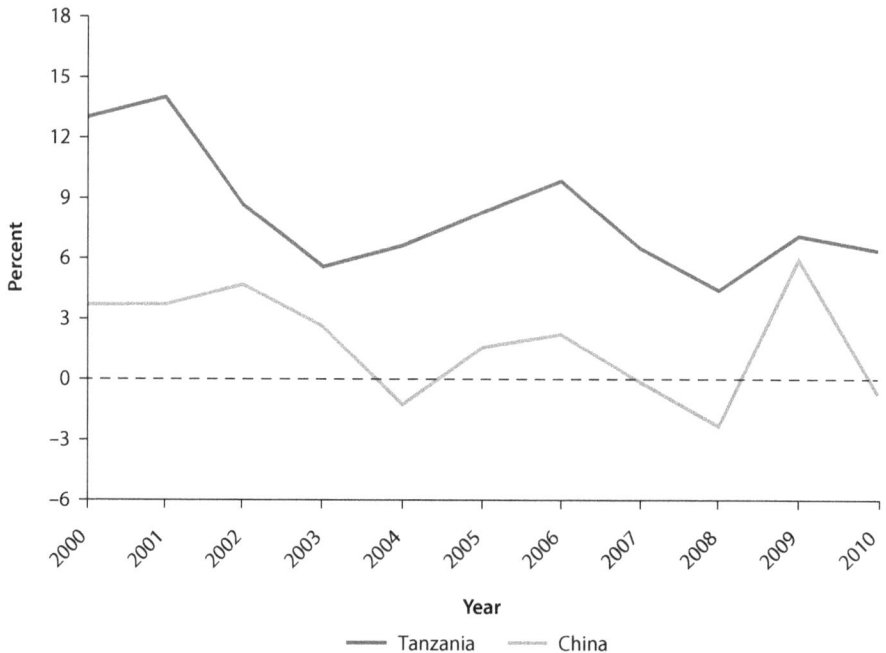

Source: IMF and World Bank 2010.

Since 2000, the real lending rate has been falling in both China and Tanzania, but it has been considerably higher in Tanzania (figure 3.2). For example, in 2010, it was 6.40 percent in Tanzania, but only –0.74 percent in China. Tanzania's high lending rate may be explained by the high concentration in that country's loan and deposit markets and the inability of the smaller banks and newer entrants to compete effectively with the larger banks. The country's three largest banks hold around half the total banking assets, deposits, and loans, and, in total assets and loans, the share of these largest banks increased in 2003–08. A formal test of competition confirms that the system is uncompetitive and compares poorly on an international scale.

The Microeconomic Constraints

This section analyzes the microeconomic issues affecting firms, such as export incentives, trade logistics, the availability of electricity, and access to land and financing. Solving the issues in trade, land, and financing would benefit the country's ability to foster growth in light manufacturing. For example, improving access to land would resolve a critical constraint on agribusiness.

The Antiexport Bias

Tanzania has ample room to expand the production of light industries whether for export or for domestic consumption. Tanzania needs to export to regional and global markets so that it can continue to grow. This requires that the antiexport bias in the trade regime be eliminated.

Tariffs, other charges, and a variety of nontariff barriers are protecting local products from imports by making the imports more expensive in the domestic market than in international markets. This makes producing for the domestic market more profitable than producing for export and shifts resources from export-oriented sectors to import-substitution sectors. These import protections create an antiexport bias by increasing the production costs for exports, thereby reducing the competitiveness of local exports in international markets.

Tanzania has a fairly restrictive trade regime. Its overall trade restrictiveness index, a measure of tariff and nontariff barriers, is 52.9 percent, the most restrictive in the East African Community.[5] In contrast, Kenya's index is 7.1 percent, Rwanda's 14.2 percent, and Uganda's 7.2 percent. Nontariff barriers account for 84 percent of import protection.

The antiexport bias could be eliminated by lifting the import protections or by reimbursing the duties and taxes paid on imported inputs if, through an effective duty and tax drawback system, the final product of the relevant domestic production is exported. Tanzania's drawback system has serious implementation problems, and exporters receive reimbursements after a long delay or not at all.

At 134 on the World Bank's 2013 doing business index, Tanzania ranks lower than other African countries. The index number is 127 for Ethiopia and 94 for Zambia, for example.[6]

Weak Trade Logistics
Tanzania needs to reduce trade costs and improve competitiveness to facilitate trade. Making Dar es Salaam Port more efficient is particularly important. The port handles almost 95 percent of the country's maritime throughput and serves six other countries (Burundi, the Democratic Republic of Congo, Malawi, Rwanda, Uganda, and Zambia). These landlocked countries are connected to the port by two railroads, a road network, and a pipeline (from Zambia). About 40 percent of the traffic at the port is transit traffic to other African countries.

Container congestion is substantial at the terminal. Container ships must queue at the outer anchorage. This raises the costs for exporters and importers and undermines firms that need to get their goods to market quickly and reliably. The delays have caused some shipping lines to suspend services at the port.

A 20-year master plan (2008–28) to increase the port's efficiency calls for investing in capacity improvements, extensions, dredging, computerization, a single-window system for customs clearance, and training. The government is planning to develop the Bagamoyo Gateway Port to ease the cargo traffic at Dar es Salaam Port and to support regional growth. Measures to reduce congestion and delays have already cut dwell time from 20 days in 2005 to 12 days in 2011.[7] But progress in implementing the master plan has been slow.

Light Manufacturing in Tanzania • http://dx.doi.org/10.1596/978-1-4648-0032-0

Inadequate Power Supply

The power shortages in Tanzania are severe. The gap between power demand and power supply has been widening: from 2000 to 2009, power generation grew at an annual average rate of 4.2 percent, while the economy grew at 7.1 percent, and power sales for industrial use were at 10.1 percent. Peak power demand is estimated at about 833 megawatts. Although installed capacity is 1,003 megawatts, the actual stable supply is only about 600 megawatts because of several factors (CTI 2011):

- Inefficient power generation, transmission, and distribution by TANESCO, the state monopoly
- Deteriorating infrastructure and slow implementation of new projects
- A legal framework that impedes the ability of private energy investors to compete with TANESCO
- Dependence on hydroelectric power generation and the seasonal fluctuations in hydroelectric power supply

The growing shortages and long and frequent blackouts are reducing productivity and slowing growth. The gaps are projected to continue to widen in the absence of serious action plans.

The power system master plan for 2010–33 calls for substantial investment in a range of energy sources, with an emphasis on transforming the country's rich natural gas reserves into power generation through public-private partnerships. Completing the necessary investments will take time, but can be realized in three to five years. Meanwhile, many private companies are importing power generators to maintain a steady source of electricity for production. However, the costs to companies for generating their own power, coupled with rising gas prices, are boosting production costs and hurting competitiveness, particularly among small and medium enterprises (SMEs). The government should thus accelerate the implementation of the planned investment and rehabilitation (CTI 2011). Other recommended reforms include the following:

- Restructuring TANESCO to increase efficiency and eliminate power and financial losses
- Revising the Electricity Act of 2008 and speeding the implementation of the act to encourage private investment in power
- Waiving import taxes on equipment for the generation and distribution of electricity[8]

Inadequate Transportation Infrastructure

The government has made notable progress in the rehabilitation and extension of the country's road network over the past decade. However, rural roads are still in bad shape, which raises production costs in the agriculture sector. As in other East African countries, transport costs are disproportionately high on rural roads. For small farmers, the cost of transport over the first mile is often the main constraint. A World Bank report finds that transport costs per kilometer-ton are three to five times greater from the farmgate to primary markets than from secondary to wholesale markets located in country capitals (Arvis and others 2010). Thus, about 45 percent of average transport charges occur during the first 28 percent of the transport distance. Railways play a crucial role in connecting the hinterland to main cities and providing access to cargo. However, the quality of the railway lines is rather poor. Dar es Salaam Port, which accounts for over 75 percent of Tanzania's international trade, is heavily congested. The air transport infrastructure is operating beyond capacity. Various reforms aimed at improving the regulatory environment have not yet remedied these problems, nor do they support private sector growth.

The government launched phase 1 of the ambitious 10-year Transport Sector Investment Program in 2007. The program aims at improving transport significantly, but, because of the escalating costs of road construction, the 2012 phase 1 targets could not be reached. The Five Year Development Plan (FYDP) was adopted in 2011 as a key implementation tool to achieve the intermediary targets of the Tanzania 2025 Vision.[9] The overarching theme of the FYDP is the unleashing of Tanzania's growth potential, with a focus on establishing the requisite business environment for sustainable high growth and on stimulating investment and trade. As key priorities, the plan identifies enhanced productivity and the provision of basic infrastructure to facilitate easy access to productive resources and markets.

The FYDP includes the construction and rehabilitation of over 5,200 kilometers of new or existing roads to appropriate standards along the main transport corridors. The plan also envisages the expansion of cargo handling capacities at the country's seaports and lake ports by 2015/16 (mainly through large investments in Dar es Salaam Port) and reductions in the total dwell time of containers at port yards (from 12.5 to 7.0 days). The government has also planned the upgrading of the port at Mtwara, the construction of a new port at Bagamoyo, and expansion of the capacity of Dar es Salaam Port. The FYDP envisages the rehabilitation of existing railway lines (especially the central line), the construction of the Isaka–Kigali line, and the preparation of feasibility studies on the construction of new railway lines connecting strategic parts of the country. The FYDP likewise aims at expanding Tanzania's air cargo and passenger freight handling capacities as part of the strategy of transforming the country into a regional and international trade gateway.

The authorities recognize that additional investments will not be sufficient to improve transport systems. The benefits of shorter travel times will not materialize if long waiting times at Tanzania's ports, airports, and railway stations and multiple roadblocks on the roads continue to cripple the efficiency of the road network. Other measures will be needed to improve administrative effectiveness and reduce regulatory burdens. Coordinating and linking infrastructure investments to policy reform are essential.

Lack of Entrepreneurial Skills and Business Development

Business surveys in Tanzania tend to highlight the perceived weakness in entrepreneurial skills for business development. Indeed, survey results point to the substantial likelihood of business failures and the inability of most local firms that survive to grow beyond a certain size or to link up with powerful international networks. The growth identification and facilitation approach suggested by Lin and Monga (2011a, 2011b) and Lin (2012) recommends that developing-country governments should adopt nondistortive policy measures whereby the state can facilitate the establishment or development of competitive industries by domestic entrepreneurs. This is particularly important in African countries where local entrepreneurs have difficulty linking with global supply chains and other business networks from which they could derive managerial expertise, learning, and financing opportunities.

To help address some of these problems in coordination and externalities, the government could encourage firms in target countries that are losing competitiveness, most notably because of rising wages, to invest in these industries in Tanzania given that such firms have the incentive to relocate their production to lower-income countries so as to reduce their labor costs. The government could also set up incubation programs to assist the entry of private sector domestic firms into these industries.[10] Potential incubation programs to foster the development of agribusiness in Tanzania could be explored with investors all over the world, but especially in Arab countries, where there is a strong demand for fruits and vegetables from Africa, and in East Asia, where the relevant technology and expertise are available.[11]

Recent empirical studies show that many countries have targeted foreign direct investment (FDI) on certain sectors of the economy selectively and quite successfully. The results of the 2005 World Bank Census of Investment Promotion Agencies, which covered over 100 countries, show that sectoral targeting is considered best practice by investment promotion professionals (Harding and Javorcikr 2007). The reason seems to be that more intense efforts that are concentrated on a few priority sectors are likely to lead to greater FDI flows relative to nontargeted, across-the-board attempts. Tanzania has recorded a steady increase in FDI inflows over the past decade.

The authorities should also pay attention to spontaneous self-discovery by private enterprises and provide support to scale up successful private innovations in new industries. Unexpected opportunities for Tanzania may arise from the country's unique endowments through technological breakthroughs around the world. This is a particularly delicate endeavor and requires utmost caution: the government should not fall into the trap of reactivating old industrial policies that relied on subsidies and protection to encourage firms to enter industries that were inconsistent with comparative advantage or ignored hard budget constraints. The incentives provided by the government to first movers should be temporary and limited and should be aimed solely at compensating for the information externalities. Through such an approach, pervasive rent seeking and the persistence of government interventions beyond the practical time frame can be avoided. A key to ensuring that government resources are not hijacked by politically powerful or well-connected business networks is the rigorous and transparent implementation of a policy framework for identifying, selecting, and supporting successful firms that have emerged in competitive industries.

Our study (Dinh and others 2013) finds that the best industrial policy is not to pick winners, but, rather, to back winners, meaning that the government should follow the lead of the private sector in picking industries and products to support, work closely with the private sector to find the most critical constraints affecting the growth of the industries and products that have been picked, and design policies to remove these constraints.

Lack of Access to Finance and the Absence of Venture Capital

Lack of access to finance: Access to finance appears to be the most binding constraint across sectors, particularly among smaller companies wanting to expand capacity to take advantage of economies of scale, invest in new technology, and train employees to increase productivity. The financing constraint contributes greatly to the missing middle (the failure of small firms in developing countries to grow to medium firms). The evidence shows that smaller companies that have access to external funds grow much more quickly than companies that have to rely mainly on their own funds for investment. For example, 80 percent of the SMEs surveyed in Tanzania had used retained earnings to finance their most recent purchase of machinery and equipment (Fafchamps and Quinn 2012). Meanwhile, during 2006–10, only 3 percent of companies in Tanzania borrowed from financial institutions, compared with about 60 percent in China and Vietnam.

The main reasons for lack of access to financing are weak bank capacity to assess small loans, inadequate bookkeeping and financial recordkeeping by firms, lack of collateral, weak creditor rights, and cumbersome contract enforcement procedures that debtors can use to delay proceedings, thereby discouraging loans and loan turnover. The costs and collateral requirements are much greater among companies in Tanzania that can borrow than among counterpart companies in China. SMEs in Tanzania pay an average annual interest rate of 14 percent, compared with about 5 percent in China.

Lack of collateral severely limits the access to credit among SMEs. Real estate (buildings and land) and salaries are normally used as collateral in Tanzania, disadvantaging SMEs. More than 70 percent of small firms lease their premises, and many micro and small companies squat in areas not reserved for businesses. Also, the fully secured lending requirements include 125 percent collateral, which is beyond the means of small companies. A large share of the microcredit supplied by commercial banks and microfinance institutions is based on payrolls. Interest rates on these loans are high, and repayment periods are short. The loans are small, and their benefit is limited.

There are serious difficulties in using land as collateral because only 11 percent of all land in the country has been surveyed (see below). The government has been conducting land and building surveys, developing land registries, and issuing titles (rights of occupancy) that may be used as collateral for credit. However,

Light Manufacturing in Tanzania • http://dx.doi.org/10.1596/978-1-4648-0032-0

progress has been slow, and activities have focused on disjointed plots of land rather than on a national-level approach. The implementation of these reforms should be greatly accelerated.

We recommend two main policy reforms to address these issues, as follows:

- Collateral system reforms should include the quick completion of land and building surveys, registration, and titling; the introduction of a movable collateral framework to encourage financing by smaller companies against their movable assets (including machinery, equipment, household assets, motor vehicles, inventory, and accounts receivable); strengthening and scaling up credit guarantee schemes; and the establishment of a credit reference bureau and a collateral registry.[12]

- A reform of the legal system could substantially improve access to credit information and the protection of creditor rights by granting exclusive jurisdiction over the enforcement of creditor claims to commercial courts and by comprehensively reforming civil procedures to reduce delaying tactics by debtors, including by limiting the number of appeals (IMF 2010).

The financial system and venture capital: The Tanzanian financial system has been stable in recent years despite the global crisis, and it has been generally supportive of the modern economic sector.[13] Financial intermediation has remained relatively smooth and strong given that it has been supported by ample liquidity and orderly conditions in domestic financial markets and in the payment and settlement systems. However, the modern sector is still insufficiently developed, and the majority of households, informal firms, and SMEs have difficulty obtaining funding from formal financial institutions. Only 17.3 percent of the population (age 15 or above) have an account at a formal financial institution, compared with nearly 63.8 percent in China, 40.0 percent in neighboring Mozambique, and 21.4 percent in Vietnam (table 3.3). While a much larger proportion of citizens in Tanzania save money (over 40 percent), less than 12 percent do so through a formal financial institution, and only 6.6 percent of the population obtained loans from such institutions in 2011.

The banking sector is adequately capitalized and liquid. As of December 31, 2010, the ratio of liquid assets to demand liabilities was 45.2 percent, which was well above the minimum regulatory limit of 20.0 percent (Bank of Tanzania 2011). The high level of liquidity in the banking sector has been attributed to a cautious lending approach among banks, which undertake significant investments in liquid government securities and also prefer to place funds abroad. The industry ratio of core capital to total risk-weighted assets and off balance sheet exposure was 18.2 percent as of December 31, 2010, which was above the minimum regulatory ratio of 10.0 percent; the ratio of nonperforming loans to gross loans had deteriorated from 6.7 percent in 2009 to 9.3 percent as of December 31, 2010, and 8.1 percent at the end of September 2011 (Bank of Tanzania 2011). The largest segment of the portfolio impairment stemmed from loans to businesses related to fishing, agriculture, mining, and tourism.

Table 3.3 Share of Population with Access to Financial Institutions, Tanzania and Selected Countries

Percent

Indicator	Tanzania	Mozambique	Cameroon	Ghana	Sub-Saharan Africa	Vietnam	China
Account, formal financial institution	17.3	39.9	14.8	29.4	24.1	21.4	63.8
For business	2.9	8.5	3.2	6.5	5.3	3.8	2.6
To receive wages	7.1	21.7	2.4	11.5	9.9	5.8	18.7
Saved money in the last year	40.1	42.6	51.9	36.6	40.2	35.3	38.4
Saved money at a financial institution	11.9	17.5	9.9	16.1	14.2	7.7	32.1
Loan from a formal financial institution, past year	6.6	5.9	4.5	5.8	4.7	16.2	7.3
Loan from family or friends, past year	46.0	35.3	45.0	28.8	39.9	31.0	25.0
Loan from informal private lender, past year	6.0	2.1	8.3	3.4	5.4	3.0	1.1

Source: Fafchamps and Quinn 2012.

Note: The table refers to the populations aged 15 years or above.

However, a follow-up examination of key banks revealed that a number of loans granted to sectors that had been affected by the global financial crisis had not been properly classified and provided for as required by the relevant prudential regulations, and the affected banks were thus directed to make appropriate adjustments (Bank of Tanzania 2011). The increase in the rate of nonperforming loans did not represent a systemic risk for financial stability and is being addressed by a strong capital buffer held by the industry. Nonetheless, the Bank of Tanzania directed the relevant banks to enhance their credit administration systems to avoid further deterioration in credit portfolios. Meanwhile, the credit risks on the assets placed overseas were limited because of the prudential regulations that required banks to spread their placements according to the credit ratings of foreign banks.[14]

The profitability of financial institutions has declined. During the year ending December 2010, the banking sector recorded declining profits after taxes to the tune of about 18.1 percent (Bank of Tanzania 2011). Industry analysts have attributed this poorer performance to the lower rate of return on assets that was recorded in 2010—3.2 percent compared with 2.1 percent in 2009—because of a deterioration in asset quality, declining returns on government securities, and reduced earnings from foreign placements in line with the declining yields on these investments.

The country's financial prospects are favorable. The most compelling evidence for this conclusion is the increasing trend in the rate of return on capital over the last two decades, albeit with considerable variation that is mostly attributable to fluctuations in price parameters such as the gross domestic product (GDP) deflator and the investment deflator. The average rate of return to capital during 1990–2000 stood at 3.5 percent and rose to 10.1 percent, on average, between 2000 and 2010.[15] This is a direct reflection of the enhanced economic performance registered over the last decade. The increase in the rate of return on capital coincided with a surge in FDI flows to Tanzania: the average annual FDI inflow rose from $120 million in 1990–2000 to $503 million in 2000–10.

However, Tanzania still lacks venture capitalists who are willing to provide funding for start-ups and small businesses with a limited operating history but with perceived long-term growth potential.[16] Such firms cannot raise funds by issuing debt. Successful businesses everywhere are often dependent upon the availability of equity capital. Bankers and other lenders generally require some equity cushion or security (collateral) before they will lend to a small business. (A lack of equity limits the debt financing available to firms.) Additionally, debt financing requires the ability to service the debt through current interest payments. These funds are then not available to grow the business. Venture capital provides businesses a crucial financial cushion.

In an environment such as Tanzania's where the capital market is still rudimentary if not nonexistent, venture capitalists would be an important source of funding for start-ups. They would differ from the financing sources available in Tanzania today by focusing on young, high-growth companies and on investment in equity capital, rather than debt. They would be more willing to take on greater risks in exchange for potentially greater returns, and they would have longer investment horizons than any of the financing schemes available in Tanzania today. They would be able to monitor closely the companies in their portfolios through board participation, strategic marketing, governance, and the capital structure. Venture capitalists in Tanzania would obviously face higher risks, but would have the potential of receiving above-average returns. They would also be able to supply managerial and technical expertise.

Difficult Access to Industrial Land

Lack of access to land is a major constraint among light manufacturers in Tanzania. Registering property takes an average of eight procedures and 68 days.[17] Many small companies are run by owners in their homes or in small workshops, often encroaching on sidewalks or public land. Such companies need land to expand and grow, and they need secure property rights so they may use land as collateral for loans. Larger companies need factory space, storage facilities, and showrooms. Without adequate storage space, companies have to purchase inputs in small quantities at retail prices rather than in large quantities at wholesale prices. They cannot satisfy large and time-sensitive orders, because they cannot stock sufficient raw materials and finished products. Without space for storage and showrooms, producers can manufacture products only to order.

Lack of access to land is also an obstacle to the backward integration of supply chains for local raw materials. The availability of accessible, affordable land is essential to commercial farms, large ranches, and private plantations in the production of high-quality agricultural products, skins and hides, and wood for light manufacturing. Adequate land is also required for affordable housing in industrial locations so that workers can avoid long, expensive commutes.

Tanzania's land management system does not meet the economy's needs. Only 11 percent of the land in the country has been surveyed, and only 5 percent is registered. Tanzania enacted important land legislation in the 1990s and the first decade of the 2000s that divided land into three categories, each with its own rules: village land (70 percent of the total, administered by village councils), reserved land (28 percent, administered under various laws), and general land (2 percent, administered by the commissioner of lands).[18] The legal framework strengthens the security of land tenure and makes land use more productive through a highly decentralized process of land demarcation, titling, registration, and conflict resolution. However, progress has been slow. An effective way to increase the area of industrial land available is to develop industrial parks and sectoral clusters with access to plug-and-play factory shells, as China and other developing countries have done. Industrial parks and industrial clusters can ease not only the land constraint, but also infrastructure, housing, financing, and other constraints as well (see below).

Competition Is Weak in Industry[19]

Formal sector manufacturing industries in Tanzania are highly concentrated. While concentration fell from 2001 to 2004, it intensified slightly in 2004–07

Figure 3.3 Average Level of Concentration, Formal Manufacturing Industries, Tanzania, 2001–07

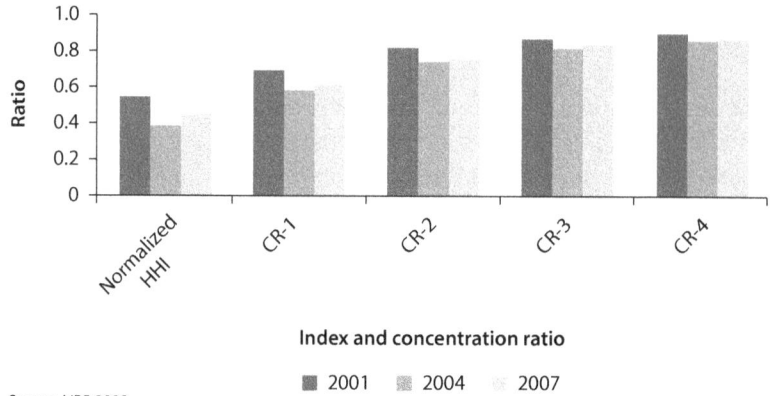

Index and concentration ratio

■ 2001   ▨ 2004   ░ 2007

Source: NBS 2008.
Note: HHI = Herfindahl-Hirschman index; CR = concentration ratio. The Herfindahl-Hirschman index is a measure of the degree to which production in an industry or in an economy is dominated by larger firms. In general, the fewer the number of firms in an industry or an economy and the more unequal the distribution of market shares among them, the larger the index. CR-1, CR-2, CR-3, and CR-4 indicate, respectively, the concentration ratios of the largest, two largest, three largest, and four largest firms in formal manufacturing.

(figure 3.3). Reversals in concentration were particularly evident in textiles, tobacco, beverages, auto parts, batteries, and machinery.

Most formal manufacturing sectors in Tanzania show high concentration indexes (such as the Herfindahl-Hirschman index), and the concentration ratios of the largest, two largest, three largest, and four largest firms (CR-1, CR-2, CR-3, and CR-4 in figure 3.3) are high. In all but a few manufacturing groups at the International Standard Industrial Classification (ISIC) three-digit level, the top three or four firms produce more than 50 percent of domestic production in their ISIC group (figure 3.4). Of the sectors highlighted in this book, food products and beverages (ISIC 15) is much less concentrated than other sectors. On the other hand, leather and leather products (ISIC 19) is highly concentrated, as is apparel (ISIC 18). Textiles (ISIC 17), wood (ISIC 20), and wood products such as furniture (ISIC 36) are at intermediate levels.

Looking at the concentration among domestic industries alone, we do not obtain the full picture because informal firms and imports contribute to competition. Nonetheless, the competition among large manufacturing enterprises is weaker in Tanzania than in other East African countries according to the World Bank Enterprise Surveys.[20] The share of large firms reporting no new competitors was much larger in Tanzania than in Kenya and Uganda (figure 3.5). Tanzanian firms also tend to be less active in international markets relative to firms in Kenya and Uganda.

There is strong international evidence that greater local competition promotes greater productivity growth because, in a competitive environment, firms invest to improve productivity to compete more effectively against each other. In Tanzania in 2006, according to World Bank Enterprise Survey data, enterprises facing less competition invested less in their products and production processes and innovated less.[21] In contrast, firms facing more competition in Tanzania

Figure 3.4 Concentration among Formal Manufacturing Industries, ISIC Two-Digit Level, Tanzania, 2007

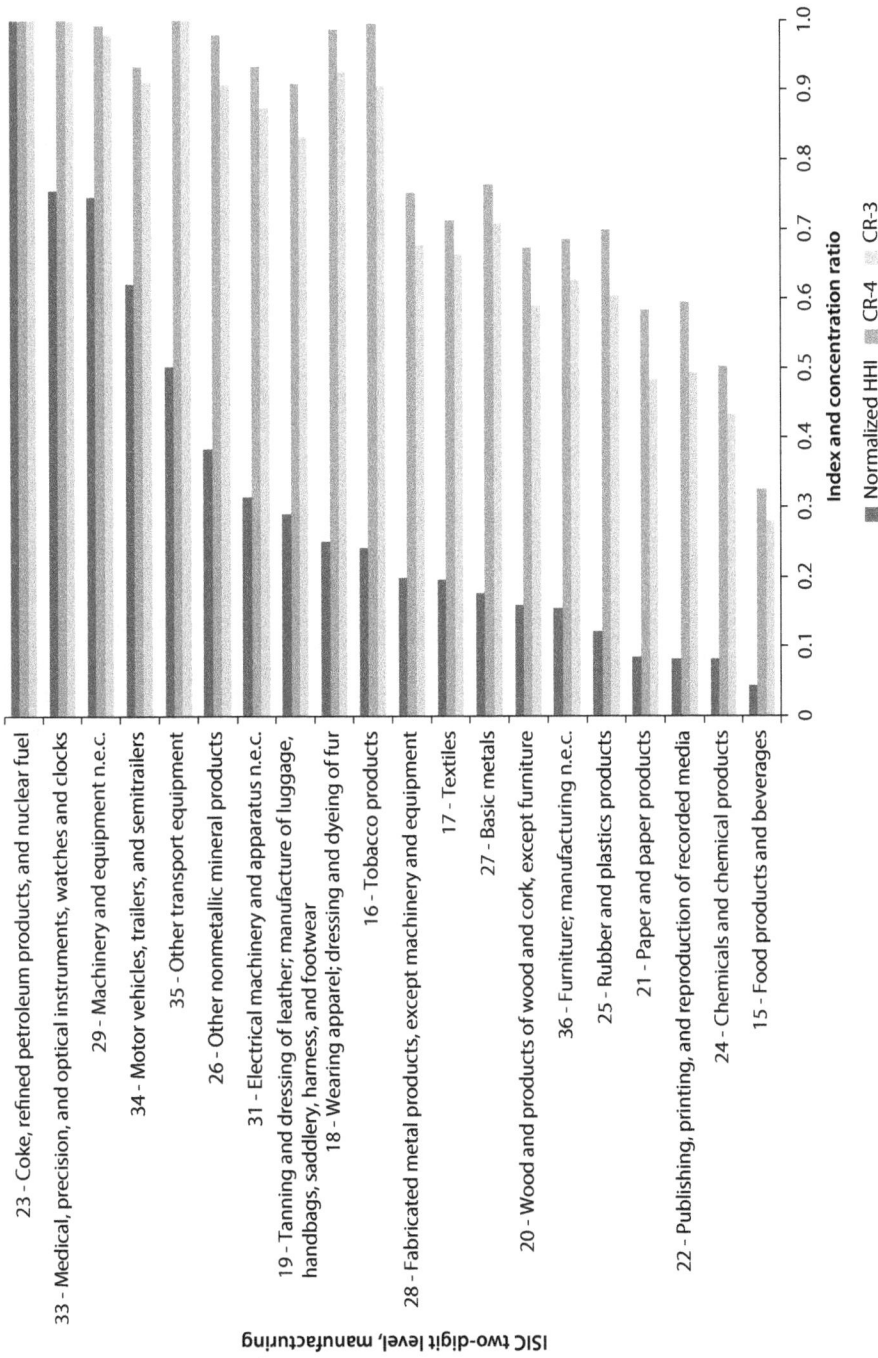

Index and concentration ratio

■ Normalized HHI ▦ CR-4 ▨ CR-3

ISIC two-digit level, manufacturing

23 - Coke, refined petroleum products, and nuclear fuel
33 - Medical, precision, and optical instruments, watches and clocks
29 - Machinery and equipment n.e.c.
34 - Motor vehicles, trailers, and semitrailers
35 - Other transport equipment
26 - Other nonmetallic mineral products
31 - Electrical machinery and apparatus n.e.c.
19 - Tanning and dressing of leather; manufacture of luggage, handbags, saddlery, harness, and footwear
18 - Wearing apparel; dressing and dyeing of fur
16 - Tobacco products
28 - Fabricated metal products, except machinery and equipment
17 - Textiles
27 - Basic metals
20 - Wood and products of wood and cork, except furniture
36 - Furniture; manufacturing n.e.c.
25 - Rubber and plastics products
21 - Paper and paper products
22 - Publishing, printing, and reproduction of recorded media
24 - Chemicals and chemical products
15 - Food products and beverages

Source: NBS 2008.

Note: ISIC = International Standard Industrial Classification of All Economic Activities. For the significance of the ISIC codes, see "Detailed Structure and Explanatory Notes: ISIC Rev.4," Statistics Division, Department of Economic and Social Affairs, United Nations, New York, http://unstats.un.org/unsd/cr/registry/regcst.asp?Cl=27.; HHI = Herfindahl-Hirschman index; CR = concentration ratio. For an explanation, see the note to figure 3.3. n.e.c. = not elsewhere classified.

Figure 3.5 The Competition Facing Large Firms, Five Countries, 2008

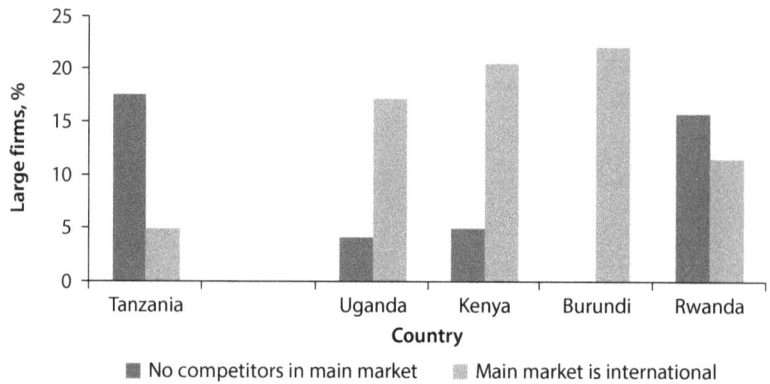

Source: World Bank 2009.
Note: The figure covers all large firms, including those not involved in manufacturing.

Table 3.4 The Link between Investment and Innovation, Five Countries, 2007
Percent

Country	Investment, as share of value added, 2007		Enterprises introducing products or processes, previous three years	
	0 or 1 competitor	2 or more competitors	0 or 1 competitor	2 or more competitors
Burundi	59.1	14.3	40.0	57.9
Kenya	3.8	13.3	70.0	80.6
Rwanda	32.0	8.5	77.8	70.8
Tanzania	31.5	43.0	53.3	81.1
Uganda	23.8	13.7	70.0	83.7

Source: Based on data of Enterprise Surveys (database), International Finance Corporation and World Bank, Washington, DC, http://www.enterprisesurveys.org.

invested more in machinery and land acquisition in 2007, on average, and had introduced more new products and new processes in their industrial activities over the previous three years than had firms in other East African countries (table 3.4).

High product-market concentration and weak competition tend to raise prices and profits because they dampen interfirm rivalry and foster monopolistic and oligopolistic business behavior, including collusion. Sometimes, structural conditions contribute to market concentration, including a small domestic market relative to the efficient scale of production; so, there is room for only a few firms. However, the adverse effects of high concentration are accentuated if domestic markets are insulated from international competitive pressures by tariffs and nontariff barriers. Therefore, policies to enhance local competition and remove anticompetitive measures against imports are a key means of broadening the private sector and raising its international competitiveness.

Competition Policy: Good Framework, Inadequate Implementation

As part of the structural reforms to establish a stronger market economy, the government enacted the Fair Competition Act in 2003. The act redesigned institutions, created new ones (the Fair Competition Commission and the Fair Competition Tribunal), and addressed many of the legal and institutional shortcomings of the previous competition regime. The main provisions of the act generally align with international best practice. However, while the legal framework for competition is well designed, implementation has been a problem, particularly in terms of integrating the regulatory and competition advocacy roles of the Fair Competition Commission. The commission can conduct research and market studies on competition and review and proffer pro-competition arguments for proposed government policies and regulations. The commission has conducted valuable research, but, based on such studies, it should intervene more directly to influence policies and regulations. Strengthening the commission's functions, particularly in competition advocacy, through adequate government budget allocations should be a priority.

Restrictive Trade Policy and Domestic Regulations

While the government has made good progress in reducing tariffs, as evidenced by changes in the country's tariff trade restrictiveness index, nontariff barriers remain. The overall trade restrictiveness index (updated in 2012) for import bundles shows that, based on the latest available data (as of 2009), Tanzania is still more restrictive than its regional peers because of nontariff barriers (see above). A World Bank regional study on nontariff barriers (2008) prepared for the secretariat of the East African Community identified the most important nontariff barriers in Tanzania. These related to customs and transport procedures, especially the limited capacity for border customs clearance, numerous roadblocks (police checkpoints), weighbridges, and tonnage restrictions. The most important product-specific barriers arise from technical and quality standards and sanitary and phytosanitary measures. Some domestic regulations, while serving other objectives, also limit competition by imposing economic costs, thereby affecting consumers.

A Shortcut: Plug-and-Play Industrial Parks

Developed and managed well, industrial parks help companies expand and improve their productivity. As China's experience with more than 1,000 industrial parks shows, successful industrial parks provide security, basic infrastructure (roads, energy, water, sewerage), streamlined government regulations (through government service centers), and affordable industrial land. They also provide technical training, low-cost standardized factory shells (plug and play), adequate free worker housing near plants, and schooling and other social services for workers and their families (Dinh and others 2012). Industrial parks can be specialized (for example, leather, textiles, furniture, or electronics) or all-purpose. Export processing zones (EPZs) are a specialized form of industrial park that allow duty-free imports of production inputs and streamline import and export procedures.

Plug-and-play industrial parks have greatly reduced start-up costs and risks among small and medium industries that are not sufficiently developed to qualify for bank loans, but that have the scale, capital, and growth prospects to take advantage of larger facilities. China's industrial parks, with government support for input and output markets, have also facilitated the development of industrial clusters, generating substantial spillovers and economies of scale and scope.

The government of Tanzania enacted the EPZs Act in 2002 and established the Export Processing Zones Authority (EPZA) in 2006. It has created both EPZ industrial parks, where investors locate their operations together in a designated zone, and stand-alone EPZs, which receive that designation from the EPZA.

In 2006, the government launched a special economic zones (SEZs) program as part of the Mini-Tiger Plan to attract foreign and domestic investment in all sectors through high-quality infrastructure, desirable fiscal packages, business and social support services, assistance in cluster formation, and minimal regulation.[22] The program includes EPZs, free ports, free trade zones, specialized industrial clusters, agricultural free zones, industrial parks for SMEs, microenterprise manufacturing parks, and information and communication technology parks. The Integrated Industrial Development Strategy 2025 (IIDS) proposes the clustering of SEZs in various locations, with an emphasis on waterfront areas in three development corridors (in Bagamoyo, Mtwara, and Tanga). Creating SEZs for microenterprises and SMEs helps alleviate the land-access problem and encourages companies to register formally. While the SEZs initially had their own administrative body, the 2011 Economic Zones Law unified the EPZ and SEZ schemes by structuring the EPZ scheme as a subset of the SEZ scheme and gave oversight authority for both programs to the EPZA.[23] In November 2012, the government adopted SEZ regulations to implement the 2011 act for the unified EPZ-SEZ regime. The regulations clarify the roles of key stakeholders, including the role of the government as a zone regulator. Rather than developing zones, the government encourages private sector participation in zone development.

The EPZs and the SEZs program are at an initial stage. The government has allocated 13 sites for SEZs, but only seven have been licensed, and only one of these seven is an SEZ.[24] There are also 20 stand-alone EPZs. The EPZs employ around 10,000 people.

SEZs have been slow to develop, and they have had limited success attracting investment and creating employment, largely because of the lack of an effective institutional framework. Other shortcomings requiring remedial measures are the following (Farole and Kweka 2011):

• *Clarity of the roles and responsibility of the EPZA.* The EPZA's roles and responsibility need to be clarified. It works as both operator and developer. It operates the Benjamin William Mkapa SEZ, and its mandate includes developing on-site infrastructure, normally the responsibility of the developer. Its principle roles should be promotion and regulation, with the two clearly delineated to avoid conflicts of interest. It should attract investment in the zones, facilitate government services (including licensing, registration, utility connections, dispute settlement, and fee setting), and monitor compliance.

- *Inclusivity of the EPZA board of directors.* Of the 12 members of the EPZA board, 9 come from the public sector (minister of industries and trade, chair; permanent secretaries in the ministries of finance, energy, infrastructure, planning, water, and land; the attorney general; and the governor of the Bank of Tanzania). The three private sector members are the chair of the Tanzania Private Sector Foundation, the executive secretary of the Tanzania Business Council, and the secretary general of the Trade Union Congress of Tanzania. Private sector representation ought to be expanded to 50 percent, including zone developers and operators.

- *Coordination of implementation.* The EPZA reports through the Ministry of Industry and Trade, but is not a department of the ministry and has partial independence. This makes it difficult for the EPZA to act with authority and coordinate effectively across public sector agencies. To boost these powers, the EPZA ought to be placed under a central entity (the Office of the Presidency, the Office of the Prime Minister, or the Ministry of Finance), preferably the same ministry as the Tanzania Investment Center. Service agreements and memorandums of understanding should also be drafted with the relevant public units.

- *Budgetary autonomy.* The EPZA budget is allocated through the budget of the Ministry of Industry and Trade; as a result, the EPZA lacks sufficient, predictable, and independent budgeting authority to plan and carry out its activities. The EPZA needs independent, multiyear budgeting and the right to solicit funds directly to supplement its budget.

- *Institutional capacity for management, monitoring, and evaluation.* The EPZA's capacity to monitor and evaluate the SEZ program is weak. Technical assistance should be sought to train staff and increase their capacity to manage the program effectively.

Overcoming the Constraints to Competitiveness

Several characteristics offer promise that Tanzania could become globally competitive in apparel, leather products, and agriculture, while competing with imports in wood products:

- Substantial and growing labor-cost advantages, combined with highly trainable workers
- Potential access to competitive sources of key inputs

- A growing domestic market
- Direct access to the Arabian Sea through Dar es Salaam Port
- Duty-free and quota-free access to the European Union (EU) and U.S. markets.

Binding Constraints

High input costs reduce Tanzania's competitiveness. Despite a rich resource base, Tanzania imports most of its inputs in the apparel and leather sectors, boosting input costs. In the agriculture sector, access to inputs and services is inadequate. Poor trade logistics raise the costs of imports and exports, already high because of insufficient access to inexpensive, good-quality domestic inputs. In addition, difficulties in accessing land, finance, and appropriate skills constrain the development and expansion of SMEs.

The binding constraints to competitiveness vary by sector and firm size (table 3.5). High production costs in apparel reflect low worker skills and high management, overhead, and trade logistics costs. Input costs are a major constraint in the leather industry, including the high cost of importing leather. High material waste (20 percent) and utility costs add to input inefficiency. In the wood and wood products sector, high input prices (expensive wood) and low labor productivity are the main constraints. The low labor productivity is explained by the limited training and experience of managers and line workers, high absenteeism, outmoded equipment, and high material waste and reject costs (reflected in the worker skills column in table 3.5). Limited access to land and inadequate agricultural inputs and services, especially for SMEs, are the major obstacles in the agribusiness sector.

Policy Recommendations

Policy actions are needed in several areas to overcome these constraints and to create public goods that facilitate private sector growth, as follows:

- Developing plug-and-play industrial parks in areas with input potential is important in all four sectors we examine. The advantages are multiple: firms are provided with affordable access to industrial land, standardized factory shell buildings, worker housing, training facilities, and one-stop shops for business regulations. Plug-and-play industrial parks also greatly reduce the financial costs and risks for successful small firms.

- In the long rum, strengthening institutions is essential to overcoming the lack of access to the key inputs vital to competitiveness and growth, such as credit, land, technology, and training. Strengthening service institutions, especially the sectoral associations, is a priority for improving advocacy and technical services. However, institutional reforms take a long time to yield results. Meanwhile, there is an urgent need to grow the manufacturing sector and to create jobs through targeted policies to remove the binding constraints in the specific sectors (Dinh and others 2012).

Table 3.5 Constraints by Light Industrial Sector, Firm Size, and Importance, Tanzania

Sector	Firm size	Input industries	Land	Finance	Entrepreneurial skills	Worker skills	Trade logistics
Textiles and apparel	Small	Critical	Important	Important	Important	Important	
	Large	Important			Important	Critical	Important
Leather and leather products	Small	Critical	Important	Important	Important		
	Large	Critical	Important	Important	Important		Important
Wood and wood products	Small	Important	Important			Critical	
	Large	Important	Important			Critical	Important
Agroprocessing	Small	Critical	Critical	Important			
	Large	Critical	Critical	Important			

Source: Based on data described in chapters 4–7.
Note: Blank cells indicate that the area is not a priority constraint.

Box 3.1 Tanzania's Success in Food Goods

Azam is the most successful manufacturer of chocolate and ice cream in Tanzania. The brand is one of Said Salim Bakhresa's many companies and is one part of the Bakhresa Food Product Ltd conglomerate. Bakhresa, who began with a small restaurant in the mid-1970s, now owns a group with a turnover of more than $300 million and has a daily capacity of 2,100 metric tons of product. The Bakhresa Group has become one of the largest private sector industrial groups and one of the largest private sector employers in Tanzania. It operates in five other countries in the region.

The group has sought to move away from imports and source inputs domestically. An example is its partnership with local farmers to produce fruit for its juice division. The farmers have benefited by receiving a return on their investment. Bakhresa Food also owns its own trucks and coolers and has created its own distribution channels. This allows the group to meet transport and distribution needs and can help explain the company's high concentration in the Tanzanian market.

This example shows that the potential exists for companies in Tanzania to benefit from the country's comparative advantage and to pursue backward links for the supply chain.

- Because a key break in the value chain takes place at the primary processing stage as a result of the use of old technology, attracting FDI is important for establishing an integrated domestic production chain in each sector.
- Coordinating donor assistance is important in all four sectors, especially in strengthening business associations, setting up vocational training, and creating business incubation facilities.

Because the binding constraints vary by sector and firm size, policy makers need a clear idea about the most promising manufacturing sectors and then must identify, prioritize, and remove the most serious constraints in these sectors. Targeted policies should be selective, consistent with comparative advantage, and in line with resources and capacity. Starting small and building gradually will prepare a solid foundation for expansion (box 3.1).

Notes

1. China is not, of course, Tanzania's only competitor, but, given the inexpensive, low-quality Chinese products flooding markets in Tanzania and other African countries, it is an important one.
2. The analysis is based on in-depth interviews (including data collected on costs and productivity) at more than 106 formal medium firms in the two countries.
3. Only part of the revenue collected through the levy is earmarked to finance labor training programs.
4. Our objective is to review and compare changes in the real effective exchange rate in China and Tanzania, not to estimate any misalignment, which is defined as the difference between the equilibrium real effective exchange rate and the actual exchange

rate. The equilibrium rate is determined by the sustainable values of economic funda-
mentals, such as the terms of trade, commercial policy, productivity, and fiscal policy.

5. The trade restrictiveness index covers all goods and calculates the uniform equivalent
tariff of a country's applied tariff schedule, including preferential tariffs, and nontariff
barriers that would maintain domestic import levels. The index thus indicates an estimated degree of trade restrictiveness that includes both tariff and nontariff barriers.

6. Doing Business (database), International Finance Corporation and World Bank,
Washington, DC, http://www.doingbusiness.org/data.

7. Dwell time is the number of days a container is involved in the changeover from
one status to another, for example, from inbound unloading to empty/available or
from empty/available to outbound loading. The shorter the dwell time, the more
efficient the container utilization. See "Dwell Time," Transportation-Dictionary.org,
Bureau of Transportation Statistics, the United States Department of Transportation,
Washington, DC, http://www.transportation-dictionary.org/Shipping/Dwell_Time.

8. The government announced an Emergency Power Plan in August 2011.

9. The Tanzania Development Vision 2025, formulated by the government and adopted
in 1999, outlines five main goals that Tanzania is expected to have attained by the year
2025, namely, (a) high-quality livelihoods; (b) peace, stability, and national unity;
(c) good governance; (d) a well-educated and learning society imbued with an ambi-
tion to develop; and (e) a competitive economy capable of producing sustainable
growth and shared benefits. See "The Tanzania Development Vision 2025," Planning
Commission, Dar es Salaam, Tanzania, http://www.tanzania.go.tz/vision.htm.

10. Bangladesh's vibrant garment industry is an example of an industry that received new
energy because of foreign direct investment (FDI), in this case, through Daewoo, a
manufacturer with headquarters in the Republic of Korea, in the 1970s (see Dinh and
others 2013). After a few years, sufficient knowledge transfer had taken place, and the
direct investment became a sort of incubation. Local garment plants mushroomed in
Bangladesh, and most of them could be traced back to that first Korean firm (Rhee
1990). Chile's successful salmon industry is an example of government incubation.
Fundación Chile, a public sector firm, set up the first commercial salmon-farming
operation in the country in 1974 and demonstrated that salmon farming could be successful in the country. The industry expanded rapidly within the private sector in the 1980s.

11. The trade links between Tanzania and the Arab world date back millennia. According
to historians, trading contacts between Arabia and the East African coast existed
by the 1st century AD, and there is evidence of early connections with India. The
coastal trading centers were mainly Arab settlements, and relations between the Arabs
and their African neighbors appear to have been fairly friendly. Early visitors to
Zanzibar and the Pemba islands included Arabs, Hindus, Jews, Persians, Phoenicians,
and, possibly, Assyrians. Swahili is the national language of Tanzania, and about one-
third of Swahili words are said to be derived from Arabic.

12. With the support of the Facility for Investment Climate Advisory Services, Ghana, the
Lao People's Democratic Republic, Liberia, Malawi, and the Republic of Yemen
recently introduced the movable collateral framework, with good results. For details,
see FIAS (2011).

13. Studies by the Bank of Tanzania show that the risk of contagion associated with the
global financial crisis did not affect the financial sector in Tanzania because of the
slight, mostly indirect exposure of the country's financial institutions to counterparts
in global financial markets (for instance, see Bank of Tanzania 2011). Even parent
banking groups had limited access to the foreign exchange reserves of their Tanzanian

subsidiaries because of the independent nature of the licensing system. Foreign banks are registered and licensed in Tanzania as legal entities that are independent of their foreign parent banking groups. This regulatory arrangement reduces the risk of repercussions from the poor performance of parent banking groups, and any potential credit losses in the event of widespread sovereign defaults are also reduced.

14. In addition, banks are required to monitor the risks involved in their foreign exchange holdings (including placements abroad) and to report on this issue to the central bank on a daily basis.

15. The calculation of the capital share in income is challenging in Tanzania. Most studies estimate the share as the residual of the labor share of income, but this method is difficult in Tanzania because of the large informal sector. Over 70 percent of the population is employed in agriculture, and the majority earns nonwage income. We use 35 percent as the capital share of income and assume a standard depreciation rate of 5 percent. We calculate the investment deflator as the weighted average of the depreciation rate and the national price index. See Monga and Mpango (2012).

16. Venture capital is a type of equity financing specially designed to address the funding needs of entrepreneurial companies that, for reasons of size, the amount of assets, and the stage of development, cannot seek capital from more traditional sources, such as public markets and banks. Venture capital investments are generally made in cash in exchange for shares and an active role in the invested company.

17. See Enterprise Surveys (database), International Finance Corporation and World Bank, Washington, DC, http://www.enterprisesurveys.org.

18. In Tanzania, the president owns the land, but citizens can obtain occupancy rights. There are two rights of occupancy. First, the granted right of occupancy can be held outside village lands, and it may be granted for up to 99 years. Land has to be surveyed before a certificate of occupancy can be issued. Second, customary right of occupancy can be held in rural areas indefinitely. The relevant certificates are issued by village councils after the land has been surveyed.

19. This section has been prepared by Yutaka Yoshino, senior economist, Poverty Reduction and Economic Management II, Africa Region, World Bank.

20. See Enterprise Surveys (database), International Finance Corporation and World Bank, Washington, DC, http://www.enterprisesurveys.org.

21. See Enterprise Surveys (database), International Finance Corporation and World Bank, Washington, DC, http://www.enterprisesurveys.org.

22. Planned with the support of the Japan Development Institute as part of the Tanzania 2025 Vision, the Mini-Tiger Plan 2020 aims at fostering the competitiveness of Tanzanian products on global markets and promoting exports, including through the creation of SEZs.

23. For detailed information about the programs, including the investment incentives and the responsibilities of the EPZA, see the website of the authority, at http://www.epza.co.tz.

24. The 13 SEZ-designated sites are Bagamoyo (Coast Region), Kitengule/Karagw (Kagera), Kiyegeya (Morogoro), Lindi Township (Lindi), Luwawasi-Mkuzo (Ruvuma), Malula (Arusha), Mererani (Manyara), Neema (Tanga), Sanya Station (Kilimanjaro), Sistila (Mbeya), Tairo/Bunda (Mara), Ujiji (Kigoma), and Usagara (Mwanza). The seven licensed zones are Benjamin William Mkapa SEZ (the only SEZ), Global Industrial Park, Hifadhi EPZ, Kamal Industrial Park EPZ, Kisongo EPZ, Millennium Business Park, and Vector Health EPZ.

References

Arvis, Jean-François, Monica Alina Mustra, Lauri Ojala, Ben Shepherd, and Daniel Saslavsky. 2010. *Connecting to Compete 2010: Trade Logistics in the Global Economy; the Logistics Performance Index and Its Indicators*. World Bank, Washington, DC.

Bank of Tanzania. 2011. *Financial Stability Report*. September, Financial Sector Stability Department, Bank of Tanzania, Dar es Salaam, Tanzania.

CTI (Confederation of Tanzania Industries). 2011. "Challenges of Unreliable Electricity Supply to Manufacturers in Tanzania." Policy research paper submitted to the Energy Sector Stakeholders in Advocacy for Ensured Reliable Electricity Supply to Tanzanian Manufacturers, CTI, Dar es Salaam, Tanzania.

Dinh, Hinh T., Vincent Palmade, Vandana Chandra, and Frances Cossar. 2012. *Light Manufacturing in Africa: Targeted Policies to Enhance Private Investment and Create Jobs*. Washington, DC: World Bank. http://go.worldbank.org/ASG0J44350.

Dinh, Hinh T., Thomas G. Rawski, Ali Zafar, Lihong Wang, and Eleonora Mavroeidi. 2013. *Tales from the Development Frontier: How China and Other Countries Harness Light Manufacturing to Create Jobs and Prosperity*. With contributions from Tong Xin and Pengfei Li. Washington, DC: World Bank.

Fafchamps, Marcel, and Simon Quinn. 2012. "Results of Sample Surveys of Firms." In *Performance of Manufacturing Firms in Africa: An Empirical Analysis*, edited by Hinh T. Dinh and George R. G. Clarke, 139–211. Washington, DC: World Bank.

Farole, Thomas, and Josaphat Kweka. 2011. "Institutional Best Practices for Special Economic Zones: An Application to Tanzania." Trade Policy Note 25, World Bank, Washington, DC.

FIAS (Facility for Investment Climate Advisory Services). 2011. *2011 Annual Review*. Washington, DC: World Bank.

GDS (Global Development Solutions). 2011. *The Value Chain and Feasibility Analysis; Domestic Resource Cost Analysis*. Vol. 2 of *Light Manufacturing in Africa: Targeted Policies to Enhance Private Investment and Create Jobs*. Washington, DC: World Bank. http://go.worldbank.org/6G2A3TFI20.

Harding, Torfinn, and Beata Smarzynska Javorcikr. 2007. "Developing Economies and International Investors: Do Investment Promotion Agencies Bring Them Together?" Policy Research Working Paper 4339, World Bank, Washington, DC.

IMF (International Monetary Fund). 2010. *United Republic of Tanzania: Financial System Stability Assessment Update*. IMF, Washington, DC.

IMF (International Monetary Fund) and World Bank. 2010. "Financial Sector Assessment Program Update: Tanzania Update Aide Memoire." IMF and World Bank, Washington, DC.

Lin, Justin Yifu. 2012. *New Structural Economics: A Framework for Rethinking Development Policy*. Washington, DC: World Bank.

Lin, Justin Yifu, and Célestin Monga. 2011a. "Growth Identification and Facilitation: The Role of State in the Process of Dynamic Growth." *Development Policy Review* 29 (3): 264–90.

———. 2011b. "Rejoinder." *Development Policy Review* 29 (3): 304–09.

Monga, Célestin, and Philip Mpango. 2012. "Creating New Jobs in Tanzania: A Growth Identification Approach." Background paper, Light Manufacturing in Africa Project, World Bank, Washington, DC.

NBS (Tanzania, National Bureau of Statistics). 2008. "Tanzania Annual Survey of Industrial Production and Performance, 2008." NBS, Dar es Salaam, Tanzania.

Rhee, Yung Whee. 1990. "The Catalyst Model of Development: Lessons from Bangladesh's Success with Garment Exports." *World Development* 18 (2): 333–46.

World Bank. 2008. "Non-Tariff Measures on Goods Trade in the East African Community: Synthesis Report." Report 45708-AFR (October 10), World Bank, Washington, DC. http://siteresources.worldbank.org/INTAFRREGTOPTRADE/Resources/EAC_NTMs_Report_Oct_10_2008.pdf.

———. 2009. "An Assessment of the Investment Climate in Tanzania." World Bank, Dar es Salaam, Tanzania.

———. 2012. *The Little Data Book on Financial Inclusion 2012*. Washington, DC: World Bank.

Sectoral Analyses

The chapters in part 2 detail the strengths, shortcomings, and recommended solutions for Tanzania to become competitive in the four light industrial sectors we examine: textiles and apparel, leather and leather products, wood and wood products, and agroprocessing (chapters 4–7). They identify the main sector-specific constraints and recommend policy measures to remove the constraints, some in the short term and others in the medium or long term. (See appendix A for a matrix of recommended actions. The institutional support structure for each sector and a diagram of the value chain for illustrative products are shown in appendix B.)

The emphasis in the chapters is on the factors that determine Tanzania's potential in light manufacturing (low labor costs, rich natural resources, a growing domestic market, and preferential access to major global markets) and on the current structure of the country's manufacturing sector (large trade deficits in sectors with latent comparative advantage, incomplete domestic value chains, and small manufacturing enterprises).

The measures we propose cannot all be implemented at once, but need to be introduced sequentially in smaller packages. For maximum impact, selected binding constraints should be identified and addressed as a package in 12- to 18-month increments and with full institutional and financial resources. The reform process should be continuous and should continue until structural transformation is achieved. As some measures become fully implemented, newer ones should be introduced to address the remaining binding constraints.

The packaging and sequencing of reforms will vary across the sectors and over time depending on the specific constraints and local conditions in the sectors. In all cases, however, successful implementation of Tanzania's industrial development strategy will require effective public and private institutions and strong coordination (chapter 8).

Experience shows that several factors of implementation contribute to successful structural transformation. These include building a high-level reform team, partnering with the private sector, mobilizing the support of development partners and civil society, and beginning with small pilot initiatives and then evaluating processes and results rigorously before scaling up successes or terminating failures.

Most importantly, the transformation must start now. Competition is heating up in other countries (Bangladesh, Cambodia). Tanzania and the rest of Africa cannot afford to miss another opportunity. While one should recognize that the task will not be easy, Tanzania does possess advantages, and, to claim success, the country must confront challenges directly.

CHAPTER 4

Textiles and Apparel

Tanzania is a major cotton producer and has the potential for building a large, integrated textiles and apparel sector. The sector is highly labor intensive. The value chain from cotton to apparel is long, and the potential for value added is 500–600 percent. Tanzania's garment exports to the European Union (EU) and the United States are eligible for duty-free and quota-free access under the EU Everything But Arms Initiative (subject to fairly liberal rules of origin) and the U.S. African Growth and Opportunity Act (AGOA).

However, Tanzania has not been able to capitalize on these opportunities. Its textiles and apparel sector remains small, and the sector's share in the country's manufacturing output is falling. This may be explained in part by the broken cotton-to-apparel value chain and in part by the poor performance of the final product industry. Tanzania locally processes only 20 percent of its own cotton after ginning, and it exports the rest. The small processing industry, especially at the final product stage, produces few, largely low-quality products and depends heavily on imports. The processing industry is not competitive because it relies on old technology, lacks technical and management skills, and faces other constraints (see below).

The textiles and apparel sector has played an important role in the industrialization of many countries. Tanzania has a latent comparative advantage in the sector, which has the potential to contribute substantially to light manufacturing, industrialization, employment creation, and poverty reduction in both rural and urban areas. The detailed comparative value chain analysis conducted for our study shows that Tanzania has the potential to become globally competitive in apparel, thanks to several factors (GDS 2011):

- A large, underemployed workforce and a large and growing labor cost advantage: Wages in Tanzania are half those in China and almost as low as those in Vietnam. Including nonwage labor costs in China widens Tanzania's potential advantage.
- Trainable workers: Tanzanian workers in the few firms that export are able to match the quality of the exports of other countries. Although productivity is low, short-term training offers great potential for boosting productivity.

- Direct access to the Arabian Sea through Dar es Salaam Port, which is being expanded and upgraded: Dar es Salaam Port represents a huge potential to address the logistics challenges and to optimize Tanzania's cost advantage over other African countries.
- Good climate and soil conditions: These are favorable for developing a competitive cotton textiles industry.
- Duty-free access to the EU and U.S. markets.

This chapter highlights the constraints and challenges at each stage of the value chain—from cotton production to spinning, weaving, and garment manufacture and export—and outlines the policies needed for Tanzania to realize its potential in textiles and apparel.

While the textiles and apparel industries are linked, the development of each industry requires different technologies and skills. Many developing countries try to develop an entire supply chain all at once and often fail, especially if the country is at an early stage of economic development. The best strategy, as shown by the East Asian countries, is to focus first on the apparel industry, which requires less skilled labor and less capital-intensive technology than the upstream activities in the value chain such as spinning or weaving. Tanzania has the potential eventually to support a strong, integrated textiles industry, but it may be more sensible in the short term to rely on foreign direct investment (FDI) to invest in upstream activities such as spinning and weaving. Policies to promote these activities can be applied later when the available levels of skilled labor and capital have become sufficient.

Structure of the Sector

The cotton-to-apparel value chain in Tanzania now lacks multiple links, and the processing component is small and noncompetitive.

Cotton Production

Tanzania is the fifth largest cotton producer in Africa. Cotton is produced by more than 400,000 mostly smallholder farmers and ginned by 77 registered firms (only 33 of which are active). In processing, the country has 19 medium and large textile and apparel companies employing about 22,500 people (table 4.1).[1] The dominant textile product manufactured in Tanzania is lightweight, 100 percent cotton printed kanga and kitenge cloth (widely used among women in East Africa). Seven of the production companies are large, fully integrated operations that spin yarn, weave fabric, print designs, and output final products. Two foreign-owned companies make garments for export. Tanzania imported about $90 million worth of apparel products in 2009, including worn clothing ($40 million), and exported roughly $70 million worth of products, mainly printed fabric or other processed textiles used in furnishings and blankets.

There are a large number of cotton producers, and the industry is competitive. Production is variable because farmers, lacking credit for inputs, move in and out

Table 4.1 Structure of the Textile Industry, Tanzania, 2010

Company	Spinning	Weaving	Knitting	Kanga, kitenge, and kikoi cloth[a]	Bed linen	Blankets	Bednets	Thread	Cloth	Made-up	Jobs
21st Century Sisal	✓	✓								✓	400
21st Century Textile	✓	✓			✓						1,300
A to Z Textile			✓	✓			✓		✓		7,500
African Pride Textile				✓							150
Afritex	✓	✓		✓							1,000
Blanket and Textile						✓					100
Ellen Knitwear			✓						✓		100
Friendship Textile	✓	✓		✓	✓						1,200
Jambo Spinning	✓										150
Karibu Textile				✓							600
Kibotrade									✓		45
Kilimanjaro Blanket						✓					100
Mbeya Textile	✓	✓		✓	✓						775
Mnzava Fabrics									✓		600
Morogoro Canvas Mill	✓	✓								✓	1,300
Mwanza Textile	✓	✓		✓	✓						1,100
New Tabora Textile	✓										445
Nida Textile	✓	✓		✓	✓			✓			1,700
Sunflag Tanzania	✓	✓	✓	✓	✓		✓		✓		1,900
Total	11	9	3	9	6	2	2	1	5	2	22,500

Source: MIT 2011.

a. A *kanga* is a garment worn by women in East Africa; a *kitenge* is an African garment similar to the sarong; and a *kikoi* is colored cloth used as clothing and wrapped around the shoulders or the waist and legs.

Table 4.2 Comparative Performance Indicators among Major Cotton Producers, Africa

Country	Price premium,[a] US$/kg lint	Competitiveness,[b] US$/kg lint	Producer share of free on truck lint price[c]	Production cost,[d] US$/kg lint	Average yield,[e] kg/ha
Benin	2.2	—	0.67	—	1,079
Burkina Faso	2.2	1.05	0.66	0.37	1,041
Cameroon	4.4	0.99	0.68	0.31	1,150
Mali	0	1.15	0.65	0.45	1,000
Mozambique	−4.4	0.80	0.50	0.38	349
Tanzania	−4.4	0.83	0.68	0.21	585
Uganda	2.2	0.93	0.70	0.31	—
Zambia	8.8	0.78	0.59	0.32	668
Zimbabwe	6.6	0.85	0.58	0.26	742

Source: Tschirley, Poulton, and Labaste 2009.
Note: — = not available.
a. Weighted average premium over Cotlook A index, 2007.
b. Free on truck costs/free on truck revenue, 2007.
c. 1995–2005.
d. Farmgate to free on truck, 2007.
e. Average yield, 2003–07.

of cotton production according to the price they anticipate, much as they do with other cash crops. Cotton lint production varied from 44,000 to 131,000 tons over 2006–11. The yield and quality are low compared with most African cotton producers. For example, the price premium—an indicator of quality—is −$4.4 per kilogram of lint compared with $8.8 in Zambia, and the average yield is 585 kilograms per hectare compared with 1,150 kilograms in Cameroon (table 4.2). The low yield and quality arise because of inadequate extension services, poor input provisioning, and the lack of credit services provided by the government and by the weak farmers association, the Tanzania Cotton Growers Association. Nonetheless, the cost of lint production in Tanzania is the lowest among African producers, and Tanzania is therefore competitive with other African producers. Tanzania exports about 4,000 tons of organic cotton lint annually, making it the fourth largest global producer after India, Turkey, and Syria.

Spinning
Tanzania has 11 mills that have a spinning capacity: 10 produce cotton yarn and 1 spins sisal fibers (see table 4.1) (MIT 2011). Most of the spinning machinery is old. Two companies (Jambo Spinning and New Tabora Textile) sell yarn in both local and export markets, while the others produce woven fabrics with their yarn. New Tabora Textile exports yarn to Colombia, Portugal, South Africa, and Turkey.

Weaving
Nine companies weave fabrics: eight weave cotton, and one weaves sisal. These companies are integrated mills that use their own yarn in fabric production. Until recently, most of the companies operated narrow shuttle looms, but many have upgraded to broader, shuttleless looms by importing 5- to 10-year-old second-hand machinery.

Garments

There are five large garment producers. Two (Sunflag Tanzania and Mnzava Fabrics) produce knitted and cloth products for export. They import some inputs, including fabric and most of the garment trims (such as zippers, buttons, fasteners, labels, undyed thread, and linings).

As our analysis shows, garment exporters in Tanzania cannot rely on the quality of locally available fabric (GDS 2011). First, there is only one domestic supplier of knit fabrics. Second, fabric quality is poor. The shrinkage rate of local knit fabrics averages 9.5 percent, compared with a more normal rate of 5 percent for fabric used for export-grade garments. This suggests that Tanzanian fabrics are not finished properly. (In general, higher shrinkage rates are indicative of the overutilization of starch and the underutilization of chemicals during finishing.) Also, the local fabric supplier offers a limited range of fabric widths from which to choose relative to imported fabric, which can be ordered in many different width variations depending on the order, design, and client needs. Although the local knit fabric is generally cheaper ($7–$8 per kilogram) and costs less to transport to the factory (average $0.04 per kilogram), garment producers in Tanzania purchase fabrics exclusively from abroad for the assembly of polo shirts to fill export orders. Typically, Tanzanian garment exporters order fabrics from the Arab Republic of Egypt, Mauritius, or European countries at prices ranging from $8.7 to $9.2 per kilogram and at transport costs of $1.3–$2.0 per kilogram depending on the order size and means of transport.

The inability of the local textile industry to supply materials at competitive prices and quality is therefore one of the key impediments in the garment industry. Local garment firms must rely on imports, although this weakens their supply chain in many respects, including the critical one of delivery time. It takes Chinese firms approximately 30–45 days to complete an order. The corresponding number is approximately 65 days among Tanzanian firms. The selection and importation of the inputs, including fabrics with the appropriate color, texture, and design features, take time.

Markets

Most of Tanzania's textile products are sold locally as kanga and kitenge (types of African clothing), and there is a large market for these products. Kanga and kitenge are also exported, particularly to Burundi, the Democratic Republic of Congo, Kenya, Malawi, Mozambique, Rwanda, Uganda, and Zambia. While the low-income segment of the local garment market sells primarily imported secondhand clothing, the high-income segment sells high-quality imported garments. Local production cannot compete with these imports, which are superior in design and quality. In many cases, they are also cheaper despite a 25 percent import duty.

Garment Exports

The export-oriented garment sector in Tanzania is extremely small and shrinking. As of January 2011, there were only four purely export-oriented garment firms in the country, and they employed few people (estimated at fewer than 2,000). The overall industry employs an estimated 14,000 people. The potential for Tanzania to expand employment in the apparel industry is enormous. Vietnam, with a population about twice that of Tanzania, employs more than 1 million people in this industry. Despite preferential access to the EU and U.S. markets, Tanzania's garment exports to these markets are limited. For example, Tanzania's exports to the United States under AGOA were valued at only $1.2 million in 2009 (mainly cotton garments and canvas products) compared with Kenya's $195.4 million.

The Main Constraints

The value chain analysis conducted on polo shirt production in China, Ethiopia, Tanzania, and Zambia for our study shows that Tanzania has the highest production costs of the three African countries: roughly $5 for each export-quality shirt. These high costs reflect challenges related to worker skills, logistics, input costs, and the inability of Tanzanian firms to generate sufficient orders to offset the high cost of inputs, management, and other overhead (figure 4.1).[2]

Production Costs

The analysis of major production costs in China and Tanzania shows why Tanzania's costs are higher (figure 4.1; table 4.3):

Figure 4.1 Cost to Produce a Polo Shirt, Tanzania Relative to China, 2010

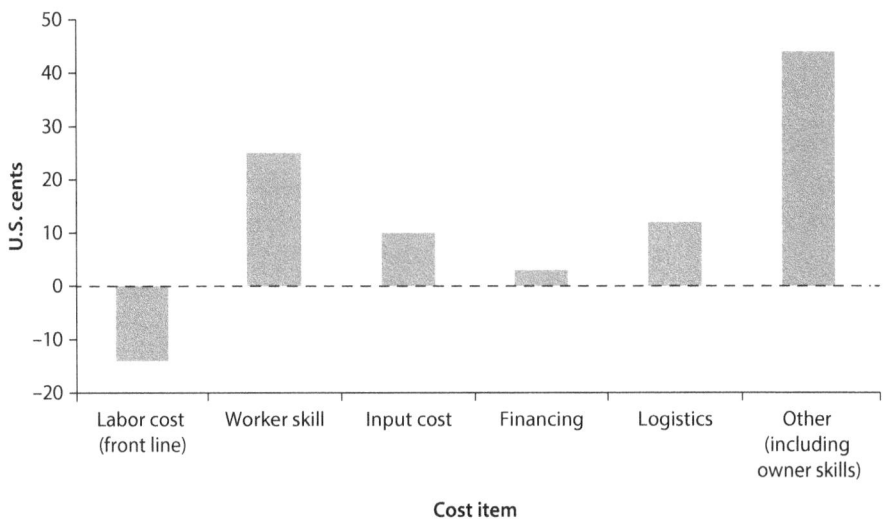

Source: GDS 2011.
Note: Here, worker skills cover labor efficiency. Other includes owner skills and utility cost and usage, as well as overhead and regulatory costs.

Table 4.3 Key Variables, the Production of Polo Shirts, China and Tanzania, 2010

Variable	China	Tanzania
Spoilage and rejection rate, %		
In-factory product rejection	2–3	1–3
Product rejection by client	0	0
Electricity		
On-grid cost, US$ per kilowatt hour	0.13	0.14
Off-grid cost, self-generated, US$ per kilowatt hour	—	0.22
Time off grid per month, %	0–10	20–30
Productivity and efficiency		
Labor productivity, pieces per employee per day	25	12
Transport, US$ per ton-kilometer	0.27–0.30	0.04–0.06
Factory		
Capacity utilization, %	60–85	50–75
Labor absenteeism, %	1	15–21
Average age of major equipment, years	1–3	8–15
Average wage per month, US$		
Skilled	311–370	107–213
Unskilled	237–296	93–173
Cost and selling price, US$ per piece		
Unit production cost	3.93–4.33	4.76–5.10
Free on board price	5.38–5.80	5.70–6.30

Source: GDS 2011.

Labor Costs

Adjusting for differences in the hours worked (the labor force in China works almost 50 percent more hours each year relative to the labor force in Tanzania), absenteeism, and in-kind benefits (for example, Chinese workers are provided with free housing), and assuming all else is equal, we find that lower wages give Tanzania an average $0.14 advantage over China in the manufacture of a polo shirt (free on board, or f.o.b., price). This wage advantage is expected to rise in absolute terms (even if wages eventually grow more quickly in Africa than in China).

Worker Motivation and Skills

Lower labor efficiency incurs a $0.25 disadvantage per shirt on Tanzania relative to China. The higher Chinese productivity derives not from differences in technology (all countries rely on similar technology), but from better skills and greater motivation in China: Chinese workers are provided with inexpensive food and with housing close to the workplace and so are able to save most of their wages. For social and health reasons, Tanzanian firms have more supervisors and higher worker absenteeism (18 percent) relative to Chinese firms. The absenteeism problem seems to be associated with worker motivation because the customary remuneration policies in Tanzania do not provide sufficient incentives, while the need for more supervisors may be attributed to the lower worker skills. The efficiency gap is expected to narrow with the continuing influx of good-practice companies and management, greater exposure to global markets, and higher capacity utilization in Tanzania.

Input Costs (Adjusted for Quality)

Raw materials (such as fabric, collars, thread, and buttons) account for more than 70 percent of polo shirt production costs. Most inputs for an export-quality shirt cannot be sourced in Africa. This imposes a $0.10 disadvantage per shirt on Tanzania relative to China because of the additional trade logistics and financing costs and the longer delivery time in Tanzania. For this calcula-tion, we assume high volumes and good trade logistics in both countries. However, for Tanzania, the penalty deriving from the need to import inputs is increased by the low production volumes, which means that producers cannot fill a 20-cubic-foot container. Differences in the cost and use of utilities do not have much of an impact on the relative production costs in China and Tanzania: utility costs (mainly electricity) are less than $0.02 per shirt. Electricity from the grid is slightly more expensive in Tanzania ($0.14 per kilowatt hour) than in China ($0.13) and also less reliable (25 percent off-grid time), for a $0.01 penalty per shirt (see table 4.3). Electricity is also more expensive in Tanzania than in Ethiopia and Zambia ($0.06 per kilowatt hour) and less reliable as well (companies rely on generators for up to 20 percent of the time, at a cost of $0.40 per kilowatt hour). Not only does energy raise the cost, but, because of its undependable nature, it makes any productivity gains more challenging.

Financing Costs

The greater investment risks in Africa result in higher financing costs (higher rates for bank financing) and higher expected returns on equity investments. Because capital investments are relatively small in the apparel sector, the impact of the higher financing costs on total production costs is less than $0.03 per shirt (assuming a hefty 10 percent risk premium—25 percent in Africa compared with 15 percent in Asia—on a $500,000 investment for a plant with an annual capacity of 1.5 million shirts). The cost of working capital and trade financing is also higher as a result of long trade delays and high fees on letters of credit.

Trade Logistics Costs

Higher trade logistics costs are the most important investment climate issue affecting the competitiveness of African apparel. Poor trade logistics in Tanzania incur a $0.12 disadvantage per shirt relative to China, almost wiping out Tanzania's labor cost advantage, and also lead to uncertainty and long delays, which result in significant price discounts from global buyers and cut Tanzania out of the main global supply chains. Tanzania is thus confined to small market niches. Tanzania exports some higher-value specialty polo shirts (with f.o.b. prices similar to prices in China), but these are small-volume products that generate orders as small as 1,000 pieces per style (standard orders run between 15,000 and 60,000 pieces). Small orders lead to higher input costs, lower capacity utilization, and higher overhead costs. It costs almost three times as much in Tanzania ($1,370) as in China ($520) to import or export a container, and it takes 31 days to clear an imported container in Tanzania. The main issues are inefficiencies at customs and high port-handling fees.

Other Costs

Much higher overhead costs impose about a $0.40 penalty per shirt on Tanzania because of the small scale of the operations and the expensive management, typically expatriates from Kenya or Malaysia. Because Tanzania does not have enough full-service industrial zones or clusters, firms require more people to manage the premises (for security, for example) and more administrative staff to sort orders.

Taxes and regulations are not much of a burden for exporters (as they are for domestic players) in any of the countries studied. China's support for its exporters (a 16 percent rebate on the exported price of apparel) offsets the preferential market access given to African countries through AGOA and the Everything But Arms Initiative.

Higher machine and building costs in Tanzania (about 25 percent higher than in China) incur only a $0.01 penalty per shirt in Tanzania relative to China because the share of capital in the production cost is low in this labor-intensive industry (10 percent of value added, including financing). To produce 1.5 million polo shirts a year (two shifts), it takes 60 flat machines, 25 cover stitch machines, and 25 thread-overlocking machines, each costing about $1,150, with a 10-year life expectancy. About 2,000 square meters of factory space is required for this production, costing about $300,000, with a 20-year life expectancy. So, even though the machines are about 25 percent more expensive in Tanzania than in China, the penalty per shirt is low.

The lower capacity utilization in Tanzania (60 percent) relative to China (80 percent) incurs a $0.01 capital-efficiency disadvantage per shirt on Tanzania. The lower capacity utilization arises because of the irregular flow of orders in Tanzania, which is not plugged into the main global apparel supply chains.

The cost of importing a 20-cubic-foot container in 2011 was $1,475 in Tanzania, lower than the average of $2,492 in Sub-Saharan Africa, but higher than the $545 in China and $645 in Vietnam (Dinh and others 2012). Tanzania's poor showing in trade logistics can be attributed to difficulties in port and terminal handling ($400 compared with $80 in China), customs clearance ($250 compared with $70), and preparation of documents and letters of credit ($520 compared with $250). In particular, Tanzania's manufacturing is centered on Dar es Salaam, meaning that inputs must be transported from upcountry regions (Mwanza, Shinyanga, and others), some 1,000 kilometers away. Transportation costs are also high because of the lack of competition in trucking, the absence of railways, and the high fuel taxes. It costs more to ship to the United States from

Dar es Salaam than from China. Because of the traffic congestion at Dar es Salaam Port and the lack of competition in shipping, shipping to Europe costs about the same in Tanzania and in China despite Tanzania's greater proximity to European ports.

Tanzanian garment firms could reduce input costs by, for example, ordering one 20-foot-equivalent-unit load of fabric per order instead of ordering only a fraction of a load (reducing fabric input costs 15–20 percent).[3] Increasing capacity utilization from 60 to 85 percent would reduce production costs by an estimated 10 percent by spreading fixed costs across higher volumes of production.[4] Combined, these two cost savings from increased volume would reduce production costs by at least 16 percent, to a total of $4.27 per polo shirt. Small and medium Tanzanian garment export firms have not been able to meet the challenge of securing large orders, partly because their limited capacity (up to 550 pieces per day) and limited product range are not appealing to foreign clients operating in the volume segment or working with multiple product and fashion cycles.

In addition to their small size, Tanzanian garment exporters face other challenges, including a lack of country awareness on the part of international apparel buyers and delivery times longer than those of Asian competitors. Tanzanian garment exporters operate in a small industry; therefore, they are attractive only to small buyers specializing in a few products. They are, however, able to execute the low-volume, high-price strategy well by selling high in the niche markets in which they operate. The value chain analysis shows that Tanzanian f.o.b. prices are among the highest among all the countries surveyed ($5.70–$6.30 per shirt). Experienced, expatriate management is a factor behind the high quality of the polo shirts produced in Tanzania, as reflected in the high price of the shirts.

Other Constraints among Small Firms

The qualitative and quantitative surveys also uncovered constraints that are particularly binding for small and medium enterprises (SMEs):

- *Lack of domestic input industries (particularly textiles):* Tanzania has an ample supply of cotton, but there are few spinning and ginning firms, and they export a large portion of their cotton lint. Little knitting is done in the domestic market, and most apparel accessories (such as buttons) are imported. The Tanzania-China Friendship Textile Company is contemplating heavy investment to modernize and integrate production to serve apparel manufacturing. Firms in China do not need to make such investments because the domestic supply is ample and importing inputs is easy.

- *Difficulties in accessing financing and industrial land among small firms* (larger firms have preferred access to both): Small firms have constrained space, and their ability to expand is limited by difficulties in obtaining financing to buy land and buildings and to upgrade machinery (Fafchamps and Quinn 2012).

The fragmented land market, with inflated prices and long transaction delays, exacerbates the problem.

- *Weak entrepreneurial and worker skills:* This prevents domestic firms from plugging into the global supply chain. The global apparel market demands rapidly changing designs; so, apparel producers need to be closely linked to buyers and must be able to adapt production designs to the quality and design preferences of the global market. There is no specialized training institution to help keep up with changing technology and other market requirements. The quantitative survey conducted for our study shows that small entrepreneurs in Tanzania have less access to skills and information than their Asian counterparts (Fafchamps and Quinn 2012). Good-practice entrepreneurs in both Asia and Tanzania have demonstrated that low-skilled workers can achieve high productivity with proper incentives and a few weeks of on-the-job training.

Policy Recommendations

Tanzania's latent comparative advantage in the garment industry indicates that the potential exists to rebuild a strong, integrated textile industry. Quantitative analysis shows that Tanzania has a strong comparative advantage in apparel. The domestic resource cost (DRC) for a polo shirt, a representative product, is 0.61, demonstrating a substantial comparative advantage and the capability of trading competitively against Chinese goods in global markets (GDS 2011).[5] Efficiency is helped by relatively low waste (1–3 percent) and rejection rates (0 percent) (see table 4.3).

Addressing the critical constraints of labor costs and inefficiencies is a priority. The government could encourage companies to reduce labor absenteeism by experimenting with variations in the piece-based wage system. Most companies try to encourage regular attendance by the workforce by establishing a fixed salary and a performance-based bonus system. For example, a typical garment firm in Dar es Salaam pays roughly $70 a month in fixed wages and an additional $20–$50 a month in performance bonuses, depending on the worker's meeting productivity targets. Nonetheless, roughly 2 in 10 workers do not show up for work on any given day.

Several steps can be taken to lower logistics costs. Rehabilitating the railroads from Dar es Salaam to Mwanza could reduce transport costs and delays. Opening trucking to new entrants (including foreign companies) and creating a level playing field for domestic companies would boost competition. Lowering the fuel tax and import tariffs on trucks and spare parts would reduce the f.o.b. production cost for manufactured goods by about 0.5 percent. Developing a plug-and-play industrial park near input production centers (for example, in Mwanza and Shinyanga, where most cotton is grown) would reduce transport costs 3 percent and cut up to 10 days from the delivery time. Both China and Vietnam started their successful apparel industries by setting up industrial zones next to world-class ports.

To deal with other, less-binding constraints, Tanzania could facilitate access to inputs (beyond improving trade logistics) through three sets of measures:

- *Eliminate import tariffs on apparel inputs* (currently 10–35 percent): Only exporters have duty-free access to inputs, and duties are levied on all inputs used in final goods that are not exported. Eliminating the duty would enable exporters to resell their material waste (reducing production costs by 1 percent) and facilitate links between large exporters and small domestic producers. This would increase productivity and output growth among small players, give exporters more flexibility to meet large orders, and facilitate the implementation of a green customs channel for apparel, another inexpensive and beneficial reform.

- *Reduce the gap in the value chain:* Preliminary evidence suggests that Tanzania could develop a competitive textile industry by taking advantage of its climate and soil conditions, which are favorable for cotton production. This would require encouraging investment in spinning and weaving to reduce import dependence. Because these industries are capital-, technology-, and skill-intensive, attracting FDI (preferably in partnership with local capital) and strengthening skills training are essential to making these segments of the value chain competitive. The priority for Tanzania would be to develop the garment sector first, while seeking to attract FDI into the earlier stages of production.

- *Develop plug-and-play industrial parks in areas with input potential* (in addition to the Bagamoyo master planning process, which can provide space for apparel and garments): China has shown that industrial parks can solve several constraints simultaneously by providing firms with affordable access to industrial land, standardized factory shell buildings, worker housing, training facilities, and one-stop shops for business regulations. Plug-and-play industrial parks greatly reduce financing costs and risks for more productive small firms, allowing them to grow into medium enterprises before they are sufficiently secure financially to obtain bank loans. This is how China has avoided the missing middle problem.

Once a program of plug-and-play industrial parks is in place, government agencies should promote Tanzania among leading global apparel investors as a destination for investment. In addition to providing immediate infusions of capital, foreign exchange, and technical, managerial, and marketing expertise, substantial foreign investment can trigger major externalities, as Daewoo did for Bangladesh by training a new generation of apparel entrepreneurs.

Notes

1. The annual industrial production surveys conducted in Tanzania cover only large industrial establishments. Therefore, data are not available for micro and small enterprises employing fewer than 10 people, such as small workshops and repair shops, an estimated 97 percent of the manufacturing firms in the sector.

2. This analysis does not pertain to the two large garment exporters in Arusha that are vertically integrated and employ more than 2,000 people each.

3. This estimate is based on an actual cost quotation from Mauritius fabric suppliers: sea freight costs of $1.30 are waived for any order of a 20-foot-equivalent-unit load of fabric, and a 10 percent discount is given on fabric prices for repeat orders of a full load.

4. This is based on a simulation of actual production costs for the polo shirt producer illustrated in the value chain analysis, that is, the costs of additional button openings and the attaching machines required in this particular factory to accommodate increased volumes are minimal (less than $0.01 per polo shirt) and are not included. The labor costs for operating the additional machines are also minimal ($0.01 per polo shirt), though these are included.

5. The domestic resource cost (DRC) is an indicator of the efficiency with which a country's domestic resources, such as labor and capital, are converted into products (see chapter 1, box 1.1). It is the ratio of the true economic cost of these domestic resources to value added measured in world prices, which are an indicator of the true economic value of internationally traded resources. If the DRC ratio is less than 1, the value of domestic resources used in production is less than the value added, and the country has a comparative advantage. If the DRC ratio is greater than 1, the value of domestic resources used in production is greater than the value added, and the country has a comparative disadvantage.

References

Dinh, Hinh T., Vincent Palmade, Vandana Chandra, and Frances Cossar. 2012. *Light Manufacturing in Africa: Targeted Policies to Enhance Private Investment and Create Jobs.* Washington, DC: World Bank. http://go.worldbank.org/ASG0J44350.

Fafchamps, Marcel, and Simon Quinn. 2012. "Results of Sample Surveys of Firms." In *Performance of Manufacturing Firms in Africa: An Empirical Analysis*, edited by Hinh T. Dinh and George R. G. Clarke, 139–211. Washington, DC: World Bank.

GDS (Global Development Solutions). 2011. *The Value Chain and Feasibility Analysis; Domestic Resource Cost Analysis.* Vol. 2 of *Light Manufacturing in Africa: Targeted Policies to Enhance Private Investment and Create Jobs.* Washington, DC: World Bank. http://go.worldbank.org/6G2A3TFI20.

MIT (Tanzania, Ministry of Industry and Trade). 2011. *Integrated Industrial Development Strategy 2025.* MIT, Dar es Salaam, Tanzania.

Tschirley, David L., Colin Poulton, and Patrick Labaste, eds. 2009. *Organization and Performance of Cotton Sectors in Africa: Learning from Reform Experience.* Washington, DC: World Bank.

CHAPTER 5

Leather and Leather Products

Tanzania has a livestock population of 34 million head (18.0 million cattle, 12.5 million goats, and 3.5 million sheep). However, the value chain is broken, and there is only a small downstream production industry.[1] The government has been trying to revive the sector and initiated a new integrated hides, skins, and leather strategy in 2007 that was intended to boost the sector through quality improvements, cluster formation, local investment, and promotion. Indeed, leather was selected as a priority in the Integrated Industrial Development Strategy 2025 (IIDS). While there are signs of recovery, progress has been slow. Meanwhile, the government is revising the 1963 Hides and Skins Trade Act to improve the legal framework for leather and leather products.

Structure of the Sector

A vertically integrated supply chain from livestock to leather products existed in Tanzania until the downstream segment of the value chain—tanning and leather products—collapsed after ill-prepared privatization and market liberalization in the 1980s and 1990s. About three-quarters of locally produced raw hides and skins are now exported, and 95 percent of the remainder is exported after some processing. Only a small share of the raw material reaches the high-value segment of the production chain (finished leather, leather footwear, and other leather products), and the few small companies still active in this segment produce mainly for the local market, leaving Tanzania with a large trade deficit in the leather products market.

Livestock, Hides, and Skins

Tanzania has the third largest livestock population in Africa (after Sudan and Ethiopia) and has the potential to produce about 2.6 million hides and 2.6 million skins annually, though only around 60 percent of all hides and skins are currently being collected (see CIBDS 2008). The rest are discarded as defective or are used by farmers in the home or for other traditional purposes. Smallholders are the dominant producers; commercial livestock activity is limited. The government levies a 40 percent tax on exports of raw hides and skins and uses the revenue to finance the Livestock Development Fund. The principal objectives of the fund are to strengthen livestock industry institutions and undertake development activities aimed at raising livestock productivity to alleviate poverty among herders. It aims to achieve these objectives through a range of activities, including establishment of an interprofessional livestock development fund, the creation of herder groups, and staff training in extension techniques.

The hides and skins produced in Tanzania are of poor quality, for many reasons:

- Poor animal husbandry practices[2]
- Inadequate disease control
- Lack of appropriate slaughtering skills, practices, and equipment[3]
- Poor storage and preservation techniques
- Lack of grading of raw hides and skins
- The export tax
- A pricing system that does not reward quality

In Tanzania's pastoral smallholder system, farmers keep livestock mainly for milk and meat. The production of high-quality hides and skins is not a goal because the export tax cuts into profits, and grading and marketing arrangements lack transparency. To maximize milk and meat production, farmers keep their animals as long as possible; so, by the time the animals are slaughtered, the skins have suffered extensive damage. Preslaughter defects account for about 40 percent of all defects among hides and skins. About three-quarters of the production of hides and skins are exported in raw form; roughly one-third is smuggled illegally through Kenya and Uganda to avoid the export tax. The main destinations of all exports are China and Pakistan.

Tanneries
Tanzania has only seven tanneries, all of them privately owned. Most tan only to the semiprocessed leather stage (wet blue) (table 5.1). About 95 percent of semiprocessed leather is exported, primarily to China, Italy, and Turkey. Only two tanneries produce finished leather, mainly for the domestic market. One tannery has started exporting finished leather to Kenya and the United States.

Leather Products
In the final products segment of the value chain, 13 small firms are active (8 produce leather footwear) and employ an estimated 200–300 people.[4] Artisanal manufacturers dominate the shoe industry, producing low-quality shoes for the local market. Other leather product activities are also based on artisans; these focus on the domestic and, to some extent, the tourist markets. Most Tanzanians wear rubber, plastic, or artificial leather shoes (imported or locally produced) rather than real leather shoes. Only 5 percent of imported shoes are leather.

Table 5.1 Leather and Leather Product Manufacturing Companies, Tanzania, 2010

Company	Location	Leather processing			Footwear	Leather products			
		Wet blue	Crust	Finished leather		Leather goods	Gloves	Leather garments	Upholstery
Afro Leather Industries, Ltd.	Dar es Salaam	✓							✓
Asilia, Ltd.	Arusha					✓			✓
East Hides Tanzania, Ltd.	Morogoro	✓				✓			
Emta Leather Products	Mwanza				✓	✓		✓	
Himo Tanners and Planters, Ltd.	Moshi	✓	✓	✓	✓	✓	✓	✓	✓
Jaet, Ltd.	Mwanza					✓			
LAT Training and Production Center	Morogoro				✓	✓			
Late Trading Co., Ltd.	Kibaha	✓	✓	✓					
LAT Training and Production Center	Dar es Salaam				✓	✓			
Moshi Leather Industries, Ltd.	Moshi	✓	✓				✓		
P.M. Tito's (Twins)	Moshi					✓			
Phyili and Sons Leather Products	Dodoma				✓	✓			
Shah Industries, Ltd.	Moshi					✓			✓
Stecor Leather Works	Arusha	✓	✓		✓				
Tanbuzi, Ltd.	Moshi	✓							
Tesha's Leather Shoes	Pwani				✓				
Woiso Shoes, Ltd.	Dar es Salaam				✓	✓			✓

Source: UNIDO 2011.
Note: LAT = Leather Association of Tanzania.

The Main Constraints

Improved trade logistics and a more well developed input industry would strengthen Tanzania's competitive position in leather products. The following are the major constraints facing shoe manufacturing:

- *Labor costs:* If we assume all else is equal, lower wages give Tanzania a $3.50 advantage over China in the manufacture of an $18 pair of shoes (free on board, or f.o.b. price) (figure 5.1).

- *Input costs:* Tanzanian shoe manufacturers have to import inputs (leather, chemicals, glue, treads, laces, and soles), resulting in a $0.60 cost disadvantage over China per pair of shoes. In particular, Tanzanian firms have difficulty sourcing large volumes of good-quality leather locally despite an abundance of skins. Measures to discourage leather exports may backfire in the medium term by reducing the profitability of tanneries and thus slowing the development of a competitive supply chain. Importing leather would solve the issue in the immediate term at a relatively small, $0.20 penalty per pair of shoes (assuming improved logistics). Higher material waste in Tanzania (20 percent) relative to China (15 percent) results in a $0.35 disadvantage per pair of shoes for the former. Tanzania incurs the greatest disadvantage, albeit a small one

Figure 5.1 Cost to Produce a Pair of Leather Loafers, Tanzania Relative to China, 2010

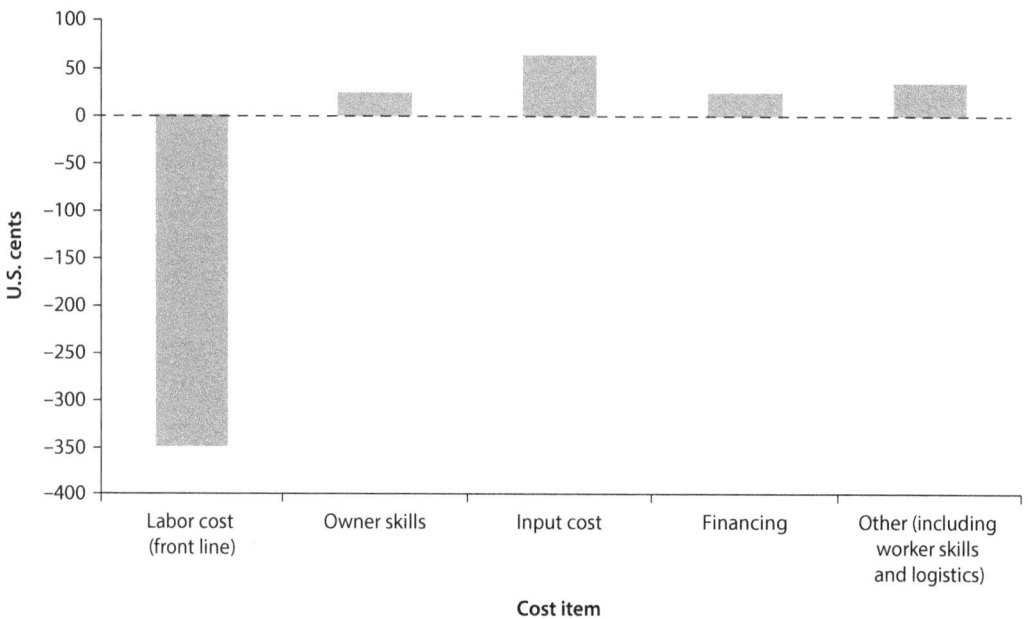

Source: GDS 2011.
Note: In the figure, worker skills cover labor efficiency.

($0.10), in electricity costs because of high electricity prices ($0.14 per kilo-watt hour) and poor-quality services (20 percent off-grid time).

- *Worker skills:* Labor efficiency in China and Tanzania is comparable.

- *Owner skills:* The share of capital in value added is even lower for shoes than for polo shirts (7 percent of value added, including financing cost). It takes $130,000 worth of machinery to produce 200,000 pairs of shoes every year in China (the main types of machines are heel nailers and setting, stitching, and slugging machines). Assuming a 10-year depreciation, this amounts to less than $0.07 per pair of shoes. In terms of capital efficiency, lower capacity utilization in Tanzania (60 percent) imposes a $0.15 disadvantage on Tanzania (with its higher capital costs).

- *Access to industrial land:* Building costs ($300,000, depreciated over 20 years) add $0.08 per pair of shoes in Tanzania. Higher capital and construction costs in Africa because of much higher land costs lead to a relatively small penalty ($0.05 per pair of shoes).

- *Financing costs:* On the basis of the same assumptions as in the case of apparel, we find that the higher financing costs in Tanzania incur only a $0.25 disadvantage per pair of shoes because the share of capital is small: a $500,000 investment (including $300,000 for the premises) for a plant that can produce 200,000 pairs of shoes a year.

- *Trade logistics costs:* No information is available on this constraint because Tanzania does not export shoes.

- *Overhead and regulatory costs (such as taxes):* China shows lower overhead costs because of clustering within industrial parks. Tanzania does not export loafers; so, no information is available on product quality, delivery, and brand and firm reputation.

Policy Recommendations

Tanzania's latent comparative advantage in leather and leather products suggests that it can rapidly create jobs in the sector. For example, leather loafers produced in Tanzania have an estimated domestic resource cost of $0.96, indicating that production in Tanzania is marginally competitive with that in China. Tanzania can improve its competitiveness substantially by removing the supply-side constraints.

Tanzania has a large domestic market. Companies in the local market will initially need to compete with imports, particularly artificial leather products. There is also a strong regional market, and Tanzania has preferential access to the major developed-country markets (see above).[5] Tanzania thus faces no significant constraints in market access and has great potential for expanding the leather products sector if it can remove production constraints at all stages of the supply chain, as follows:

- *Gradually reduce and eventually remove the export tax on raw hides and skins:* This policy aims to help the processing industry by making adequate raw materials available at low prices. The export tax does not serve the intended objective; instead, it depresses the prices that farmers receive, thereby discouraging the production of high-quality hides and skins. The processing industry needs good-quality raw materials and access to credit, skills, and technology. To avoid market disruptions, Tanzania would be better off to reduce the tax gradually as tanning technology is upgraded and leather production becomes competitive. Eventually, the export tax will need to be removed.

- *Provide technical assistance to sectoral associations:* The sectoral associations in Tanzania represent the interests of their members in dialogues with the government and other stakeholders and provide services to their members, such as training and information. Their institutional capacity and financial resources are limited, however. The Leather Association of Tanzania has been ineffective because of a lack of leadership, of commitment from its members, and of financial resources (relying largely on donors).[6]

- *Encourage new investment:* Investment in new technology in leather tanning and products is essential if the industry is to be renewed. Foreign direct investment (FDI), preferably in cooperation with local companies, should be encouraged, and industrial clusters should be formed for the leather industry. This should be supplemented by training in entrepreneurship and in management, technical, and design skills.

- *Commercialize the livestock sector:* The commercialization of the livestock industry would improve the health of livestock, the quality of the hides and skins, and the offtake ratio.[7] The government is breaking up the large state-owned National Ranching Company into smaller firms with 500- to 2,000-hectare ranches for lease. The process should be accelerated and supported by creating leather industrial clusters in appropriate locations. Encouraging the establishment of modern abattoirs would vastly improve the offtake ratio. These upstream measures would improve the quality at every stage in the value chain.

- *Enhance extension services:* Even with an effort to commercialize, most production units would remain small for the foreseeable future. To assist these units, the government should facilitate the enhancement of extension services, particularly in crossbreeding, disease control, slaughtering, preservation, and quality improvement, including in hides and skins. Donor support will be needed to launch and run these programs.

- *Improve the legal and regulatory framework:* The government is revising the 1963 Hides and Skins Trade Act. The new legislation should establish a grading and market information system on prices to ensure that farmers receive fair price for hides and skins. Enforcement mechanisms should be strengthened for regulations on slaughtering, preserving, and transporting livestock. Well-trained independent inspectors and collection center graders are also important and should be encouraged.

- *Strengthen institutional capacity and policy coordination:* Institutional capacity needs to be enhanced in both the public and private sectors. The government may need to seek donor support initially through technical assistance and financing. The activities of the many public and private institutions involved in policy formulation and implementation need to be more well coordinated. One option would be to establish a Leather Board (similar to the Cotton Board) as a regulatory and policy coordination body managed jointly by stakeholders.

Notes

1. In industrial surveys in Tanzania, the leather and textile sectors are grouped together; so, production and employment data disaggregated for the leather industry are unavailable, and accurate assessments are impossible.

2. More than 90 percent of the livestock in Tanzania are local breeds of low genetic merit that are raised within traditional pastoral and agropastoral systems.

3. In rural areas, animals are slaughtered at the homestead or at slaughter slabs. Many hides and skins are defective because of poor slaughtering skills and inadequate equipment. At the district and regional levels, animals are slaughtered in abattoirs that lack modern technology. Tanzania has only two large, modern abattoirs (Arusha and Dodoma). A few smaller abattoirs are also in good condition (Kongwa Ranch, Monduli, Mwika, Peramiho, and one being built in Dar es Salaam). The rest need upgrading.

4. Two large companies also produce nonleather footwear, such as plastic slippers and shoes, that is exported to regional markets.

5. At 0.5 pairs per person, Africa has the lowest annual footwear consumption of any part of the world; the United States has the highest, at 7.1 pairs per person (UNIDO 2009). As per capita incomes increase, demand in Tanzania and other African countries is expected to rise.

6. Other, smaller associations include the Tanzania Milk Processors Association, the Tanzania Milk Producers Development Association, the Tanzania Feed Manufacturing Association, the Tanzania Goat Network, and the Livestock Traders Association. These associations provide credit, extension services, input supplies, and marketing channels for livestock production. Professional associations—such as the Tanzania Chambers of Commerce, Industry, and Agriculture; the Agricultural Council of Tanzania; and the Confederation of Tanzania Industries—also deal with issues in the leather industry. Donors—such as the Food and Agriculture Organization of the United Nations, the United Nations Industrial Development Organization, the Common Fund for Commodities, and the Eastern and Southern Africa Leather

Industries Association—likewise prepare and finance programs, though these are usually small and not sustainable.

7. The offtake ratio is the ratio of the number of animals slaughtered over a given period (generally a year) to the total size of the herd at a given time (the number of head of livestock).

References

CIBDS (Center for International Business Development Services). 2008. "Review of Hides and Skins Marketing System in Tanzania." Report, Leather Association of Tanzania, Dar es Salaam, Tanzania.

GDS (Global Development Solutions). 2011. *The Value Chain and Feasibility Analysis; Domestic Resource Cost Analysis*. Vol. 2 of *Light Manufacturing in Africa: Targeted Policies to Enhance Private Investment and Create Jobs*. Washington, DC: World Bank. http://go.worldbank.org/6G2A3TFI20.

UNIDO (United Nations Industrial Development Organization). 2009. "Development Trends in the World Leather Products Trade." UNIDO, Vienna.

———. 2011. "Technical Report." Report YA/URT/11/A03/11-1, December, UNIDO, Vienna.

CHAPTER 6

Wood and Wood Products

In Tanzania, forests are a rich natural resource that is poorly protected and underutilized. Forests cover roughly 40 percent of the land area of the country, and hardwoods—used mainly for furniture manufacturing—are abundant. Tanzania is losing an estimated 1 percent of its forests each year to illegal logging, unregulated removal of fuelwood and charcoal, and changes in land use. Wood products are not identified as a priority sector in the Integrated Industrial Development Strategy 2025 (IIDS), and there is no integrated strategy to promote the sector. Forest- and wood-based activities are labor intensive, and an estimated 800,000 people earn their livelihoods from these activities. There is potential to improve the performance of all segments of the value chain, creating many jobs and reducing poverty.

Structure of the Sector

The wood and wood products sector includes forest resources, sawn wood production, and finished wood products. The upstream segment of the value chain (milling and furniture manufacturing) is small. Tanzania has a large trade deficit in furniture.

Forest Resources

About 70 percent of Tanzania's forested area is used for productive activities, and 30 percent is protected. Besides logs for timber, forests are a source of fuelwood, paper products, and wood-based panels and poles.[1] Almost all the forest resources in Tanzania are natural, public forests. The country's 15 production plantations (mostly softwoods, including pine) cover less than 1 percent of the forested area, but are nonetheless a good source of industrial wood. The bulk of the industrial consumption of softwoods is for the construction industry. Most logging companies are small, and their technology is old. The recovery rate in harvesting is only 20–35 percent, meaning that 65–80 percent is left in the forest as waste. The furniture sector consumes limited quantities of wood, mostly hardwoods.

To stop deforestation, the government passed the Forest Act in 2002. The law banned exports of logs greater than 4 inches in diameter (about 10 centimeters) starting in July 2004. However, enforcement was weak, and illegal logging continued. In early 2006, the government reinforced the export ban, but illegal logging (especially in the coastal forests) and exportation accelerated, resulting in the gradual extinction of many tree species in the coastal forests. Limited government capacity and governance issues have impeded enforcement. The transport of logs is particularly prone to corruption because frequent inspections of trucks during transport offer ample opportunities for bribery.

Sawmills

Sawn wood production (saw milling and hand sawing combined) commands about 70 percent of the sector's processing capacity, followed by pulp and paper production, at about 20 percent. Small sawmills with old technology, some 30–40 years old, dominate the industry. Only 11 sawmills employ more than 10 people. Mobile sawmills have recently been introduced. Waste is a problem in the milling segment of the value chain because Tanzania does not have integrated mills that use waste to manufacture other products, such as chipboard, fiberboard, and briquettes.

About 15 percent of sawn wood production, mostly hardwood, is exported semiprocessed (without kilning), primarily to China, India, and Kenya. Large furniture manufacturers in Tanzania import fully treated (kilned) timber from Cameroon, the Democratic Republic of Congo, Gabon, Mozambique, and Zambia. Long delays in Dar es Salaam Port greatly increase trade costs.

Wood Products

Used primarily in building and construction, joinery, furniture making, and packing, sawn wood is Tanzania's most important wood product. In 2008, 113 firms were operating in the wood processing sector, though only six were large (each employing more than 100 people). Of these firms, 96 were involved in manufacturing furniture and 17 in manufacturing wood, cork, straw, and similar products. The sector employs approximately 3,400 people (table 6.1). About 90 percent of the firms in the sector are locally owned.

Tanzania has a large trade deficit in wood products. In 2009, imports were valued at a total of $87 million, $66 million of which was accounted for by furniture. Exports totaled $37 million, and furniture accounted for only $3 million. The $63 million trade deficit in wooden furniture suggests there is potential for replacing imports if production can become competitive.

The Main Constraints

Producing a wooden chair costs $30 in Tanzania and Zambia and $40 in Ethiopia, but only $13 in China and $17 in Vietnam. The higher costs in Africa arise because of the more expensive wood in Ethiopia and Zambia and the much

Table 6.1 Wood and Wood Products Production, Tanzania, 2008–09

Trade and production	2008	2009
Exports, US$, millions	—	37
Wood and articles of wood	—	34
Wooden furniture	—	3
Imports, US$, millions	—	87
Wood and articles of wood	—	21
Wooden furniture	—	66
Companies operating in the sector	113	—
Furniture manufacturers	96	—
Employment in the sector	3,392	—

Source: GDS 2011.
Note: — = not available.

Table 6.2 Price of Pine Lumber, Five Countries, 2010
US$ per cubic meter

Country	Imported	Domestic[a]
Ethiopia	—	667
Tanzania	—	275
Zambia	—	394
China	—	344
Vietnam	246	146

Source: GDS 2011.
Note: — = not available.
a. Denotes the origin of the supplier, but not necessarily the source of the wood.

lower labor productivity in all three countries. Wood is cheaper in Tanzania than in China (table 6.2).

The price of wood products is higher in most African countries than in China because the former have not developed sustainable plantations of rapidly growing tree species (such as pine, acacia, bamboo, and eucalyptus). Because wood is a low value-to-weight item, improving trade logistics would substantially reduce the cost of imported wood.

The nominal wage in wooden chair manufacturing in Tanzania is less than half the corresponding wage in China, but, in labor productivity, the ratio is about 1 to 10. Chinese workers produce 4.5 wooden chairs a day, compared with 0.5 in Tanzania, 0.4 in Zambia, and 0.3 in Ethiopia. The lower wages in Africa cannot compensate for such stark differences. The low labor productivity in Africa may be explained by the age of the equipment used in furniture manufacturing (20–65 years in Tanzania, but 3–7 years in China), the limited training and experience of managers and front-line workers, and the high absenteeism (10–20 percent in Tanzania). The shortage in labor and managerial skills results in twice as much material waste: 20 percent in Tanzania and 10 percent in China, adding almost $2 to the cost per chair in Tanzania, but only $1 in China (figure 6.1). Finally, the limited expertise means a much greater use of

Figure 6.1 Major Cost Penalties, Wooden Chair Production, China and Tanzania, 2010

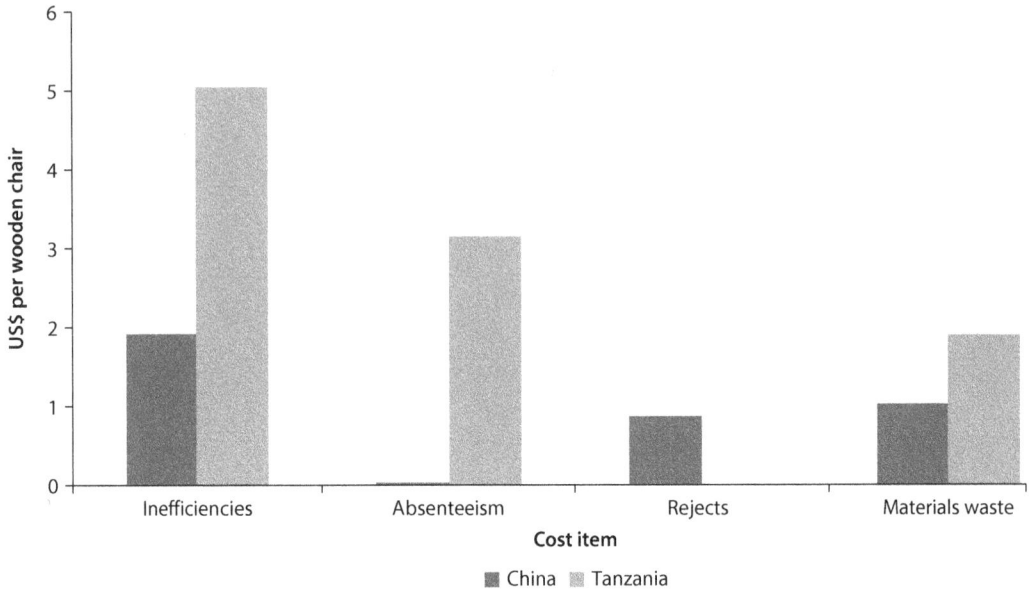

Source: GDS 2011.

consumables such as glues and varnish in Tanzania, resulting in a $4 production cost penalty per chair.[2] Another reason for the productivity differences is the scale of operations (20 times larger in China). The low capacity utilization (typically 50 percent for most furniture and seat manufacturers) and the high waste rate in production (15–30 percent in Tanzania, but 10 percent in China) also boost production costs (table 6.3). As a result, the production cost of a wooden chair is $30–$33 in Tanzania, but only $11–$14 in China.

Unlike the apparel and leather sectors, the wood products sector in Tanzania has not benefited from much technical assistance. Technical training could greatly boost the productivity of African firms, as it did among firms in Vietnam's Phú Khê village, near Hanoi, where carpenters were trained to use modern techniques to produce furniture from softwood.

In sum, Tanzania could have a competitive wood products industry by developing sustainable plantations of rapidly growing wood species and training management and workers. Improving trade logistics would also be valuable, especially while the plantations are being developed.

Policy Recommendations

The domestic resource cost (DRC) for wooden chairs in Tanzania is 2.66, indicating poor competitiveness.[3] Much of the problem arises from low labor productivity, which is explained largely by the old machinery, high labor absenteeism,

Table 6.3 Benchmarking Key Variables, Wooden Chair Production, China and Tanzania, 2010

Variable	China	Tanzania
Average spoilage		
Lumber-to-chair conversion waste, %	10	15–30
Electricity		
On-grid cost, US$ per kilowatt hour	0.13–0.15	0.14
Off-grid cost, self-generated, US$ per kilowatt hour	—	0.25
Time off grid per month, %	0–14	20–40
Productivity and efficiency		
Labor productivity, pieces per employee per day	3.0–6.0	0.3–0.7
Fuel and oil usage, liters per 1,000 pieces	14–28	385–750
Fuel and oil usage, US$ per 1,000 pieces	13–27	436–875
Factory		
Capacity utilization, %	85–100	50–60
Labor absenteeism, %	1–2	10–20
Average age of major equipment, years	3–7	20–65
Average wage per month		
Skilled, US$	383–442	150–200
Unskilled, US$	206–251	75–125
Unit production cost, US$ per piece	11–14	30–33
Average wholesale price, US$ per piece	14–17	53–60

Source: GDS 2011.
Note: — = not available.

inadequate managerial and technical skills, and frequent power outages. These factors wipe out the advantages of low lumber costs and low nominal wages. At the top end of the import price range, wooden chair production is still uneconomic, but more marginally so, at a domestic resource cost of 1.37 (GDS 2011). This indicates that wood products could be produced competitively if the key constraints on production were removed. This would require, among other steps, much more investment in modern equipment and training, reduced absenteeism, and a stable power supply, as follows:

- *Improve worker skills* through formal and informal training such as Kaizen training (World Bank 2011).
- *Encourage new investment and technology upgrades.* In all stages of the supply chain, substantial new investment is needed to replace old equipment and upgrade technology by
  - Encouraging foreign direct investment (FDI), preferably as joint ventures
  - Enhancing training for technical and modern design skills
  - Building new, integrated wood products clusters close to forested areas
- *Encourage private plantations.* Tanzania has only 15 production plantations, accounting for less than 1 percent of the country's forested area. Private

investment in plantation forestry is needed to meet the demand for fuelwood and the long-term supply of wood-based industries.

• *Develop an integrated sectoral strategy and strengthen institutions and policy coordination.* The wood products sector is labor intensive and has a long value chain with substantial value added and a latent comparative advantage. To take advantage of this potential, the government will need to develop a vision for wood products and prepare an integrated strategy to raise awareness and bring all stakeholders in the value chain together to agree on an action plan and to coordinate implementation. Institutional capacity, in both the public and private sectors, should also be strengthened through donor-supported technical assistance that enhances surveillance and promotes the sustainable use of forestry resources, tightens the enforcement of regulations, and assists companies in advocacy and other services, including training. A Wood Products Board (similar to the Cotton Board) could be established as a regulatory and policy-coordination body managed jointly by industry stakeholders to ensure coordination and promotion along the entire value chain.

Notes

1. Of the 28 million cubic meters of wood removed from Tanzanian forests in 2005, 90 percent was used for fuelwood, which accounts for about 90 percent of the country's energy use (in particular, the production of charcoal by traditional earth kiln methods). This overexploitation is causing serious degradation of the natural forests. There are 365 companies licensed to harvest softwood from an annual allowable cut of 1.2 million cubic meters, and 88 companies are licensed to harvest hardwood from an annual allowable cut of 300,000 cubic meters.

2. For example, African firms report use rates for adhesives and glues at 200–250 grams per chair, compared with 50–60 grams per chair in China and Vietnam. Africa uses varnishes and oils at 4–10 times the rate in China.

3. Data on wooden chair production are subject to considerable uncertainty. For example, the old age of the production units and the lack of reporting by unit owners of replacement capital costs mean that one must rely on imputed data, including comparisons with Ethiopia.

References

GDS (Global Development Solutions). 2011. *The Value Chain and Feasibility Analysis; Domestic Resource Cost Analysis.* Vol. 2 of *Light Manufacturing in Africa: Targeted Policies to Enhance Private Investment and Create Jobs.* Washington, DC: World Bank. http://go.worldbank.org/6G2A3TFI20.

World Bank. 2011. *Kaizen for Managerial Skills Improvement in Small and Medium Enterprises: An Impact Evaluation Study.* Vol. 4 of *Light Manufacturing in Africa: Targeted Policies to Enhance Private Investment and Create Jobs.* Washington, DC: World Bank. http://go.worldbank.org/4Y1QF5FIB0.

CHAPTER 7

Agroprocessing

Agroprocessing is the dominant manufacturing sector in Tanzania, with a 55 percent share in total manufacturing in 2008. Strengthening agroprocessing is part of the *Kilimo Kwanza* (agriculture first) policy because this would have a substantial positive impact on employment, growth, and poverty reduction in rural and urban areas. More growth in agroprocessing would encourage higher yields and result in broader markets for farmers, fewer postharvest losses, higher value added, more foreign exchange earnings, and less expensive food for Tanzanians.

Tanzania has large trade deficits in some agroprocessing industries, such as dairy products and edible oil. This implies a substantial loss in foreign exchange, as well as in potential employment and value added. To reduce these losses and realize the benefits, the government has selected a handful of agroprocessing industries—edible oil, cashew nuts, fruit processing, and milk and dairy products—as target industries in the Integrated Industrial Development Strategy 2025 (IIDS). The Tanzanian agroprocessing sector cannot grow without an expansion in agricultural production and improvements in the quality of agroproducts.

Structure of the Sector

Resource-based, labor intensive, and distributed widely throughout the country, agroprocessing has strong backward and forward links to the economy. Yet, most of the agricultural products of the country are exported without processing.

Agriculture

About a quarter of Tanzania's gross domestic product (GDP) is accounted for by agriculture, the main source of income of 80 percent of the rural population. The same share of the country's foreign exchange earnings originate from agricultural exports. Agriculture is vital to sustaining Tanzania's significant economic growth rate, its progress in poverty reduction, and its food security. It is also a major source of raw materials for agro-based industries.

A large variety of crops can be grown in Tanzania because of the country's wide variation in climate and good endowment of arable land, rangeland, and water resources. Maize, rice, and wheat are staple and commercial crops, and banana and cassava are important subsistence crops. Traditional export crops include cashews, coffee, cotton, tea, and tobacco. Other widely grown crops include beans, millet, sorghum, sweet potatoes, and an array of fruits, vegetables, oilseeds, and flowers.

Most farmers are smallholders. Productivity is low largely because of the limited use of modern technology and agricultural inputs, inadequate extension and other services, and poor infrastructure. The potential for improving agricultural productivity is considerable.

Programs have been initiated over the past few years to bring the green revolution to Tanzania. In 2006, the government, in collaboration with stakeholders, prepared the Agricultural Sector Development Program for 2006–13, a comprehensive program that supports

- Rural infrastructure, including irrigation
- Agricultural research and extension services
- Capacity building among producer associations, public sector service providers, and rural financial institutions
- Private investment in input provisioning and marketing

The program also aims to improve the regulatory framework in the agricultural sector and facilitate vertical integration by building agroprocessing clusters. A key feature of the program is the devolution of decisions on resource use to beneficiaries and local governments. The program is supported by multiple international donors.[1]

In 2009, the Tanzania National Business Council launched Kilimo Kwanza, which emphasizes the need to shift from subsistence to commercial farming and aims to facilitate private sector participation in all aspects of agricultural development, including input provisioning, marketing, and agroprocessing. Kilimo Kwanza indicates the main policy directions for implementation, but does not lay out a plan.

The Southern Agricultural Growth Corridor of Tanzania Initiative, launched in 2010, maps how private investment can promote commercial farming, a key objective of Kilimo Kwanza. The Agricultural Council of Tanzania—an umbrella organization for agricultural stakeholders—is coordinating the initiative. The growth corridor that is the focus of the initiative covers rich agricultural land and an established trade route from Dar es Salaam to the Democratic Republic of Congo, Malawi, and Zambia.[2] It aims to promote commercial farming along the corridor by

- Strengthening infrastructure, including transport, power supply, irrigation, and storage facilities
- Developing clusters to connect smallholders to agricultural businesses through contract farming

Table 7.1 Structure of the Agroprocessing Industry, Tanzania, 2008

ISIC code[a]	Activity	Firms, total	Employment		Value added	
			Number	%	Amount, T Sh, millions	%
102	Fish products	15	3,878	3.6	72,209	4.0
104	Vegetables and oils	31	1,107	1.0	32,730	1.8
106	Grain milling	61	2,205	2.1	34,510	1.9
10+	Other food products	96	36,602	34.1	339,796	18.9
11–12	Beverages and tobacco	37	12,593	11.7	404,436	22.5
13–15	Textile, apparel, and leather	47	13,430	12.5	86,971	4.8
10–15	Total agroprocessing	287	69,515	64.7	988,652	55.0
16–33	Other manufacturing	393	37,872	35.3	808,731	45.0
	Total manufacturing	680	107,388	100.0	1,797,383	100.0

Source: MIT 2011.
a. ISIC = International Standard Industrial Classification; see "Detailed Structure and Explanatory Notes: ISIC Rev.4," Statistics Division, Department of Economic and Social Affairs, United Nations, New York, http://unstats.un.org/unsd/cr/registry/regcst.asp?Cl=27.

- Improving support services among farmers
- Developing new financing mechanisms for farmers and agribusinesses

Agroprocessing

Agroprocessing is a large industry: 287 agroprocessing companies, each with 10 or more employees, contribute 55 percent of the manufacturing value added and account for 65 percent of the manufacturing employment in the country (table 7.1). More than 80 percent of the companies are small. Food products contribute more than half the value added in agroprocessing. Beverages, fish products, grain mill products, and animal and vegetable fats and oils are the largest components of the food processing segment.

The Main Constraints

The Main Constraints in Wheat Milling

Grain milling was selected as the representative sector for the quantitative analysis in our study. Tanzania has 61 producers of milled grain, starches, and similar products; these employ 2,205 people. Tanzania imports wheat and exports wheat flour. Annual wheat demand in Tanzania is about 600,000 tons, and only 10–15 percent of this is produced locally. A 35 percent import duty on wheat boosts domestic prices and stimulates domestic production.

The domestic resource cost (DRC) for wheat milling is 1.05, indicating that the sector is marginally uncompetitive.[3] If the inefficiencies detailed below are addressed, the domestic resource cost can be brought down below 1, meaning that Tanzanian wheat flour would be internationally competitive. Imported wheat accounts for about 85 percent of the total production cost of wheat milling; so, the cost is highly sensitive to the price and availability of wheat. Our value chain analysis used an import price to Tanzania of approximately $260 a ton. If the real price rises, operations would no longer be viable.

Table 7.2 Benchmarking Key Variables, Wheat Flour Production, China and Tanzania, 2010

Variable	China	Tanzania
Average waste		
Milling ratio, %	70	72–77
Electricity		
On-grid cost, US$ per kilowatt hour	0.15	0.06–0.14
Off-grid cost, self-generated, US$ per kilowatt hour	—	0.24
Time off grid per month, %	0–10	0–20
Productivity and efficiency		
Labor productivity, tons per employee per day	0.2–0.4	1.0–2.2
Electricity use, on grid, kilowatt hour per ton	9.3–14.8	57.0–65.0
Electricity use, on grid, US$ per ton	1.23–2.19	8.01–9.70
Factory		
Capacity utilization, %	95–100	60–100
Labor absenteeism, %	1–5	5–10
Average age of major equipment, years	3–8	5–10
Average wage per month		
Skilled, US$	398–442	200–250
Unskilled, US$	192–236	100–133
Unit production cost, including by-products, US$ per ton	322–377	422–433
Average selling price, wholesale, US$ per ton	273–325	448–461

Source: GDS 2011.
Note: — = not available.

Labor productivity in wheat milling is considerably greater in Tanzania than in China, and the wages in Tanzania are about half the wages in China (table 7.2). However, these advantages are outweighed by a number of inefficiencies. As a result, the unit production cost is considerably higher in Tanzania ($422–$433) than in China ($322–$377).

Despite favorable climate and soil conditions, wheat costs more in Tanzania than in China because of the poor performance in wheat farming in the former. Tanzania faces a number of challenges in producing staple crops:

- Shortages of high-yielding seeds and agricultural inputs
- Limited irrigated farming
- Entry barriers affecting large commercial farms, such as land policy issues
- Lack of appropriate storage infrastructure
- Absence of market mechanisms to support stable, predictable prices
- Lack of working capital among wholesalers

The main inefficiencies in wheat milling include the following:

- *Inefficient port services:* All imported wheat comes through Dar es Salaam Port. Millers report major bottlenecks. The charges paid to the Tanzania Port

Authority are significant, and unloading a 10,000-ton load takes about 17 days. The port's infrastructure is often out of service, and importers have to pay private companies to perform port services ($600 per day to hire a grab unloader, for example). Mandatory stevedoring charges paid to the Tanzania Port Authority are $6–$8 a ton. Port weighbridges are often out of commission or inaccurate (a 500-kilogram variance on a 10,000-ton weight is commonly reported); so, private services have to be hired (at $800 a day).

- *Labor absenteeism:* Labor absenteeism is higher in Tanzania (5–10 percent) than in China (1–5 percent).
- *Electricity availability and use:* Tanzania's unreliable electricity network reduces the productivity of mills. The electricity grid is down as much as 20 percent of the time, twice as often as in China. Electricity use is also much greater in Tanzania (57–65 kilowatt hours per ton) than in China (9–15 kilowatt hours per ton).

The much higher price of wheat in Tanzania is the primary constraint preventing the country's wheat milling industry from becoming more competitive.

The Main Constraints in Dairy Production

Though it has the third largest livestock population in Africa, Tanzania exported only $1 million in dairy products in 2009, far below China's $51 million (table 7.3). China is a major producer of dairy products, with output valued at more than $29 billion in 2009. The steady growth in China's dairy industry reflects the rapid change in the country's dietary habits, especially among urban consumers.

The average dairy farm in Tanzania has fewer than 10 cows, while the average dairy farm in China has hundreds. The cost of producing one liter of milk is

Table 7.3 Snapshot of the Dairy Industry, Five Countries, 2009

Key comparative indicators	China	Vietnam	Ethiopia	Tanzania	Zambia
Total production value, US$	29,450,322,733	530,225,356	1,118,518,519	453,000,000[a]	—
Total import value, US$	892,667,190	539,780,000	—	8,449,252	5,021,905
Total export value, US$	51,402,368	156,700,000	106,944	1,105,951	241,693
Number of operating companies	12,903	1,670	151,355	203[b]	6,128
Small, %	35.0	43.4	99.8	64.0	94.6
Medium, %	40.0	55.1	0.2	15.0	4.9
Large, %	25.0	1.5	0.0	21.0	0.5
Workers, number	9,956,316	54,795	697,793	43,792	57,200
Men, %	73.0	75.5	77.0	73.0	97.9
Women, %	27.0	24.5	23.0	27.0	2.1

Source: GDS 2011.
Note: — = not available.
a. Based on the estimated 1.7 billion liters of milk produced in 2009 and valued at an estimated $0.27 per liter.
b. Includes all formal agribusiness and food companies each with 10 employees or more; does not include an estimated 150,000 households keeping improved cattle.

Table 7.4 Average Cost of Producing One Liter of Milk, Five Countries, 2009

Country	Cost, US$ per liter	Firms benchmarked, total
Ethiopia	0.47	9
Tanzania	0.42	9
Zambia	0.52	12
China	0.25	10
Vietnam	0.22	9

Source: GDS 2011.

Table 7.5 Comparison of Local and Crossbred Cows, Africa, 2009

Attribute	Local cows	Crossbred cows
Share of total cows, %	85	15
Fat composition of milk, %	4.5–5.0	3.5–3.7
Lactation period, days	239	300
Milk yield, liters a day	1.3	12.0

Source: GDS 2011.

substantially higher in Tanzania ($0.42) than in China ($0.25) and Vietnam ($0.22) (table 7.4). Tanzanian dairy products incur a $0.12 quality penalty because the milk has less lactose and a higher somatic cell count.

Several factors explain the high cost of milk in Tanzania:

- *Low capital efficiency because of the predominance of low-yield cows:* Only 15 percent of dairy herds in Tanzania consist of high-yield, crossbred cows (table 7.5). The low yield of most cows raises the costs of milking, animal husbandry, and overhead (including veterinary services, which are a fixed cost per cow). This leads to about a $0.10 penalty per liter of milk. It is not economical to invest in efficient milking equipment and veterinary services for low-yielding cows. These cows cost about $1,000 a head, a capital cost of about $0.02 per liter, with a 15-year life expectancy.
- *Higher overhead costs of smaller herds:* Much smaller herds (combined with lower yields) lead to a $0.05 penalty per liter of milk.
- *Higher input costs because of more expensive feed:* Higher feed costs lead to a $0.02 penalty per liter of milk, a result of weakness in the wheat (see above), maize, and soybean segments and poor trade logistics.
- *Lower quality because of poor animal husbandry:* Poor animal husbandry, lack of cooling equipment, and limited recourse to veterinary services lead to lower-quality milk. The cost of veterinary services is about $0.01 per liter of milk (on high-yield cows).

The main policy issues impeding a more competitive dairy industry in Tanzania concern land and financing. Land policies limit the emergence of large farms, and access to financing is difficult for smallholders, who cannot use their land and animals as collateral.

The Main Constraints in Agroprocessing

The main constraints in agroprocessing are as follows:

- *Limited commercial farming:* Tanzanian agriculture is dominated by smallholder farms that practice mostly subsistence farming using traditional inputs and techniques and producing low yields and low-quality products. Limited access to land is a major constraint on the establishment of larger commercial farms.

- *Inadequate access to agricultural inputs and services:* Introducing modern farming techniques is challenging in a smallholder system. It is difficult to bring agricultural inputs and services to a large number of small farmers in an environment with poor infrastructure, especially with inadequate institutional capacity in the public and private sectors. Small farmers also lack the financial resources to purchase these services commercially.

- *Broken supply chain:* Tanzania exports most of its agricultural products without processing, forfeiting substantial gains in employment and value added activities. Tanzania also has large trade deficits in some agroprocessing industries, such as dairy products and edible oil. This likewise implies a loss of potential employment and value added activities, as well as a substantial loss in foreign exchange.

- *Few agroprocessing clusters:* Tanzania has only a few agroprocessing clusters. Cluster formation is a particularly effective way to address multiple constraints, including limited access to land, poor infrastructure, and cumbersome regulatory procedures and enforcement. Cluster formation is a key objective of the Integrated Industrial Development Strategy 2025, but progress has been slow.

- *Poor sanitary conditions and a cumbersome regulatory framework:* A large share of the output in food products is produced by small producers in their homes and fields under unsanitary conditions. Training services to ensure food safety are inadequate; the regulatory framework is cumbersome; and the infrastructure to support standards and management is weak. There are 17 pieces of legislation on food safety, food quality, and food quality control; these are implemented by 18 different institutions (TPSF and CCP 2010). This burdens companies with time-consuming and costly licensing and inspection procedures for food production, distribution, import, and export.

- *Lack of good-quality, affordable packaging materials:* Good-quality packaging at competitive prices with appropriate labeling is essential in marketing agricultural products. Packaging includes glass jars with metal closures, metal cans, plastic bottles, and shrink wrapping in plastic bags. Small companies in Tanzania have limited access to such packaging materials.

- *Weak sectoral associations and policy coordination:* Tanzania has only a few sectoral associations in dairy, meat, and milling. These associations are too weak in institutional capacity, skills, and finance to be effective advocates for the industry, to engage in policy dialogue with the government, and to provide services to their members. The umbrella organization, the Agricultural Council of Tanzania, lacks adequate capacity to support the other sectoral organizations.

Policy Recommendations

The main policy recommendations for the agroprocessing industry concern commercial and contract farming, cluster formation, the regulatory framework, training in food processing, and the packaging industry.

- *Facilitate commercial farming:* Under the Southern Agricultural Growth Corridor of Tanzania Initiative to promote commercial farming through increased private investment, commercial farm blocks are to be subdivided into units of 50–1,000 hectares and leased to farmers. A farm hub and outgrower scheme will include a nucleus commercial farm with storage and processing facilities connected to nearby villages over feeder roads, as well as power and water services. These initiatives require strong public-private partnerships to build the necessary infrastructure and arrange services, such as farm machinery and equipment leasing.

- *Encourage contract farming:* Contract farming could address the lack of access among small farmers to agricultural inputs and services, while formalizing the connection between smallholders and the agroprocessing industry. Zambia uses contract farming to connect cotton producers and ginners. Contract farming could be implemented in Tanzania first as a pilot scheme and, if successful, adopted more widely later.

- *Accelerate cluster formation:* Cluster formation requires collaboration among stakeholders, including local governments, the Export Processing Zones Authority (EPZA), and sector associations, to build the needed infrastructure, establish supply chain management, create training-with-production services, and develop market links. A pilot approach would also be appropriate in cluster formation.

- *Improve the regulatory framework:* The Tanzania Bureau of Standards and the Tanzania Food and Drug Authority need to be restructured and equipped with modern technology and skills to improve the management of standards, certification, and control. The Tanzania Food and Drug Authority is drafting the National Food Safety Policy, which is expected to address the numerous anomalies, duplications, and restrictions in the food industry that are impeding the industry's development.

- *Enhance training services for food production under hygienic conditions:* Several training initiatives have been established or proposed for small agroprocessing companies, including one for training in food processing and production centers at the Small Industries Development Organization (SIDO), to be financed by the Korea International Cooperation Agency. Similar programs should be developed through donor-financed technical assistance organized by various associations and the Vocational Education and Training Authority in areas where agroprocessing companies are concentrated. Training can also be conducted in clusters.

- *Encourage the packaging industry:* An assessment is needed to identify the packaging needs in agroprocessing. A feasibility study should be carried out to assess the investment opportunities in the production of packaging materials. Once this work is completed, the government could encourage foreign direct investment in agroprocessing, preferably in partnership with local entrepreneurs.

- *Strengthen sectoral associations:* Sectoral associations provide critical services to their members, including advocacy, policy dialogue, technical assistance, training in skills and standards, and market information. These associations should be fully represented on the Tanzania Agricultural Council. Policies affecting agriculture and agroprocessing are formulated and implemented by a wide range of public and private institutions. The council can provide critical policy coordination. To do this properly, the council needs to be represented at the private sector umbrella institutions, such as the Tanzania National Business Council and the Tanzania Private Sector Foundation. Substantial technical assistance should be mobilized among the donor community to strengthen the capacity of sectoral associations and the Tanzania Agricultural Council.

Notes

1. The donors include the African Development Bank, the Danish International Development Agency, the European Union (EU), the International Fund for Agricultural Development, the Japan International Cooperation Agency, and the World Bank. For details, see MAFC (2011) and the government program document, "Agricultural Sector Development Programme (ASDP): Support through Basket Fund," http://www.agriculture.go.tz/publications/english%20docs/ASDP%20 FINAL%2025%2005%2006%20(2).pdf.

2. The initiative was prepared in consultation with stakeholders including the African Development Bank, the European Union, the Norwegian Embassy, the U.S. Agency for International Development, and the World Bank. See the concept note, "Southern Agricultural Growth Corridor of Tanzania: Concept Note," prepared with the support of the Tanzania Agricultural Partnership within the Agricultural Council of Tanzania, at http://www.agdevco.com/images/sagcot_concept_note.pdf.

3. To assess the economics of wheat milling, the amount of overhead and operating costs allocated to by-products has to be considered. Based on output data from our value chain analysis, the share of bran, waste, and germ is approximately 25 percent of output in the firms surveyed. This value has been deducted from the production cost to give the net cost of milled flour.

References

GDS (Global Development Solutions). 2011. *The Value Chain and Feasibility Analysis; Domestic Resource Cost Analysis*. Vol. 2 of *Light Manufacturing in Africa: Targeted Policies to Enhance Private Investment and Create Jobs*. Washington, DC: World Bank. http://go.worldbank.org/6G2A3TFI20.

MAFC (Tanzania, Ministry of Agriculture, Food Security, and Cooperatives). 2011. "Report on the Evaluation of the Performance and Achievements of the Agricultural Sector Development Program." MAFC, Dar es Salaam, Tanzania.

MIT (Tanzania, Ministry of Industry and Trade). 2011. *Integrated Industrial Development Strategy 2025*. MIT, Dar es Salaam, Tanzania.

TPSF (Tanzania Private Sector Foundation) and CCP (Cluster Competitiveness Program). 2010. "Supporting the Competitiveness of Food Processing in Tanzania: Strategic Action Plan; Executive Summary." TPSF and CCP, Dar es Salaam, Tanzania.

CHAPTER 8

Institutional Support for Policy Coordination

Because Tanzania lacks the resources and skilled personnel to implement all sectoral and cross-sectoral reforms at once, the government ought to center its attention initially on the binding constraints identified in this book. The packaging and sequencing of reforms will vary across the sectors and over time depending on the specific constraints and local conditions in the sectors. In all cases, however, a successful implementation of Tanzania's industrial development strategy will require the assistance of effective public and private institutions and strong coordination. This chapter considers the Integrated Industrial Development Strategy 2025 (IIDS) and focuses on access to finance, training to enhance entrepreneurial and technical skills, and the institutional support and coordination necessary to promote small and medium enterprises (SMEs). These constraints are not exhaustive, but they have been prevalent in all four of the sectors we survey in this book and so should be addressed with a sense of priority.

Industrial and Sectoral Strategies

A sectoral strategy and implementation plan, prepared in collaboration with stakeholders, can establish the vision for the industrial sector by defining goals and policies and coordinating stakeholder activities. It should identify necessary sectoral and cross-sectoral reforms, including reforms in infrastructure.

Tanzania does not lack industrial strategies. As a continuation of many development plans (including the Sustainable Industrial Development Policy, the National Development Vision 2025, and the Tanzania Mini-Tiger Plan 2020), the IIDS was adopted in 2011 (MIT 2011a). It is more elaborate and specific than the previous strategies, and it includes a concrete action plan (MIT 2011b). It lays out policy steps, the agencies responsible for executing the steps, and the time frames for implementing the steps (the three five-year plans, in 2011–15, 2016–20, and 2021–25).[1] Thus, the government is preparing a detailed strategy for the leather and leather products sector based on the IIDS, to be followed by the identification of strategies aimed at the other priority sectors. While the IIDS provides a broad vision and a comprehensive action plan for industrial development, realizing it fully may not be possible given Tanzania's weak institutional capacity (see below).

Access to Credit

Policies have been adopted with the broad objective of expanding access to credit and the opportunities among SMEs in Tanzania. The most relevant recent initiative is the Economic Empowerment and Job Creation Program, which was adopted in 2006 to promote SMEs, primarily by facilitating access to subsidized credit. The program was implemented in two phases through a guarantee facility and an on-lending facility to channel the funds to SMEs. By December 2010, more than T Sh 47 billion had been disbursed to nearly 72,000 entrepreneurs and companies. However, similar to the IIDS, there has been no assessment of the effectiveness of the program in promoting businesses and no analysis of sustainability. A detailed review of the program is needed urgently, including recommendations for improvements or alternatives.

To improve access to finance among smaller companies and guide the development of the microfinancing industry, the government introduced the National Microfinance Policy in 2000. The policy encompasses guidelines for a legal, regulatory, and supervisory framework for microfinance activities (MOF 2000). The main laws governing the microfinance industry are the Cooperative Societies Act of 1991, the Bank of Tanzania Act of 1995, and the Banking and Financial Institutions (Microfinance Companies and Micro-Credit Activities) Regulation of 2005. The Bank of Tanzania includes a Directorate of Microfinance, which has a mandate to license, regulate, and supervise deposit-taking, equity-based microfinance companies. The legislation and regulations introduced under the 2000 National Microfinance Policy are being updated.

The government also created two credit guarantee schemes in 2002, one for smaller businesses, and one for agricultural exporters. Both schemes are managed by the Bank of Tanzania. Few commercial banks have agreed to participate, and the government is trying to transfer the program to a private entity.

Many more institutions have become engaged in microfinance over the last decade, including banks, nongovernmental organizations, and cooperative-based institutions.[2] These institutions offer services to SMEs mainly through microcredit, although there are also cooperative-based institutions, which are centered predominantly on equity and savings. Loans are provided to individuals or groups. Some banks, including CRDB Bank Plc, the largest banking institution in Tanzania as measured by assets, supply wholesale funds to smaller microfinance institutions, such as nongovernmental organizations, that are not permitted to collect deposits and depend largely on donor funding. Many microfinance institutions require borrowers to hold savings accounts as collateral on loans.

There are roughly 90 credit-based institutions. Around half are members of the Tanzania Association of Micro Finance Institutions, which was established in

2002 with the support of the Swedish International Development Agency. There are about 800 cooperative-based institutions across the country. Mismanaged over the years, most of these institutions have lost the trust of the public, though the government now has a program to revive them. Savings and credit cooperative societies have emerged recently as alternative microfinance solutions for meeting the rising demand in the informal credit market. The interest rates offered by these cooperatives are lower, and the loan conditions more clearly favor borrowers relative to most microfinance institutions. Compliance is easier, and the risk of default is lower because borrower savings are used as collateral. The cooperative institutions are based on membership and are more accessible to people with lower incomes. This model has rapidly become popular in both rural and urban areas but has been impeded mainly by the lack of a regulatory framework and effective management skills.

Donor Programs

Two large donor programs support SMEs. One, the Financial Sector Deepening Trust, a five-year program, was established in 2006 by the governments of Canada, Denmark, the Netherlands, Sweden, and the United Kingdom, in collaboration with the Bank of Tanzania. The program supports commercial banks and other financial institutions in the development of new microfinance products and the expansion of their outreach to underserved customers.[3]

The other, the SME Finance Innovation Challenge Fund, was created by the International Finance Corporation and implemented by the Financial Sector Deepening Trust. The fund aims to encourage financial institutions to develop new business models that will deliver new products and better services to smaller underserved business clients. This risk-sharing program may involve new technologies, better credit scoring, improved links among service providers to reach previously unserved or underserved businesses, new service channels, and creative customer service and marketing strategies. By financing up to half the cost of the development of new services, the program seeks to support financial innovation and encourage ideas that might otherwise be too risky to attract commercial operators.[4]

The National Empowerment Fund

Smaller companies are supported by the National Empowerment Fund, which is administered by the National Economic Empowerment Council and which was created through the National Economic Empowerment Act of 2004. Though not dedicated to SMEs, the fund directs a large portion of its loans to SMEs. The fund became operational in 2008 with seed capital of T Sh 400 million deposited with CRDB Bank to guarantee credit up to T Sh 1.2 billion to entrepreneurs in five regions (Lindi, Manyara, Mtwara, Rukwa, and Singida). The area covered and the value of the loans will increase as the amount of seed capital deposited with CRDB Bank grows.

In parallel with credit banking and microfinance institutions, there have been a few technology-driven initiatives to provide smaller enterprises with access to finance. Among these is the use of cell phones by households and firms to receive timely information, but also money. The rapid expansion of money transfers has been well publicized in Kenya and also in Tanzania. The reliance on cell phones helps reduce the transaction costs that are a major deterrent to the expansion of commercial credit among small-scale customers. These new channels not only facilitate credit expansion, which takes time, but also help monetize the informal economy, the first step in the development of a local financial market. Experience elsewhere shows that such supply-side initiatives must be supported by demand-side programs to improve the capacity of customers to manage finance-related information and gain access to commercial banking.

Policy Recommendations

Despite the large number of microfinance institutions in Tanzania, only about 5 percent of the potential market is covered. The institutions serve mainly urban areas. More than half the financing goes to enterprises owned by women in trade, food vending, and agriculture. Sparsely populated rural areas, where the costs and risks are high, are underserved.

The government should continue to improve the policy environment so that smaller businesses can obtain the loans they need to grow. The following actions are recommended:

• *Conduct a performance assessment:* There is no detailed assessment of the structure of the market for microfinance, the performance of microfinance institutions, or the effectiveness of government policies in microfinance. A comprehensive assessment is needed to identify weaknesses with a view to improving the design and implementation of microfinance initiatives. This assessment would also shed light on the validity of recent studies that challenge the usefulness of microfinance as a development strategy.

• *Update the microfinance policy and establish a microfinance regulatory authority:* The 2000 National Microfinance Policy does not meet the challenges small businesses face today. A new policy should cover the development of a national strategy of inclusion that emphasizes bank outreach through service centers (such as mobile vans), mobile banking, and a more effective Tanzania Postal Bank (perhaps through a strategic partnership). A microfinance regulatory authority is needed as well.

• *Expand capacity-building programs:* The current capacity-building programs in financing among SMEs that are provided by the Small Industries Development Organization (SIDO) and among financial institutions, including microfinance institutions and savings and credit cooperative societies, are limited. These programs need to be expanded to build institutional skills in the assessment and provision of small loans and to enable enterprises to maintain a financial information system so that financial institutions can determine credit risk.

Vocational and Technical Skills Training

Differences in entrepreneurial and technical skills partly explain the differences in productivity between smaller and larger companies in the same sector and between companies in Tanzania and companies in other countries. For example, in Tanzania, small companies have one-ninth the productivity of large companies.[5] Many factors drive productivity, including access to education, technology, finance, electricity, and water. In Tanzania, 70 percent of small-business owners have less than seven years of education; in Vietnam, the corresponding share is less than 5 percent. In China and Vietnam, nearly 90 percent of small-business owners have more than some secondary education; in Tanzania, this is true among only 20 percent of small-business owners (Fafchamps and Quinn 2012).

Improving skills among the labor force requires actions on both the demand and supply sides of the labor market. On the demand side, firms need to have the capacity to find the workers with the skills that match their needs. Because of the mismatch between educational outcomes and the operational skills required to be productive on the labor market, this is far from easy in Tanzania. The search costs are also high among firms in the many areas in which a formal labor market is absent and information on the available workforce is difficult to collect. In these areas, informal channels are generally relied on to locate qualified workers. The bias in favor of the application of physical capital—notably, because of general tax exemptions for investment and the overtaxation of labor—encourages firms to use physical capital rather than skilled workers.[6]

On the supply side, the education system, while improving, is still not adequate. The secondary schooling system is largely inefficient in providing students with an education that is useful in meeting the economic needs of the country. This is evident in the high number of dropouts and the relatively low rates of return associated with secondary education in Tanzania: students with a few years of secondary education do not earn significantly higher monetary incomes than students who stop schooling at the end of the primary cycle. This trap in the education system is generally recognized; it is the result of several deficiencies, including poorly trained teachers, the lack of incentives to remain in education, and the ineffective curricula. The quality of the education system is also a major issue.

On-the-job training has been a key method for teaching skills among workers in many countries. However, in Tanzania, the vast majority of firms do not provide such training to their employees. This is especially the case among SMEs, which lack the human and financial resources to develop such programs. Many SMEs also consider the provision of on-the-job training a risk because they fear the newly trained workers will quit to seek higher incomes among competitors or open their own businesses. This is a vicious circle. The experience in other countries shows that learning programs carried out within formal or informal industrial clusters represent an effective way to foster skill development, while avoiding the vicious circle because of the dynamic knowledge sharing occurring through labor-pooling in industrial clusters.

Another reason for the shortage of skilled and semiskilled workers is the lack of education and training alternatives for students who do not wish to continue in postsecondary education, which is attained by less than 5 percent of the population in Tanzania. More vocational and technical training programs are needed to nourish the market for lower-skilled workers and technicians.

The government has taken some steps to fill this gap.[7] Thus, the Vocational Education and Training Act has led to the establishment of the Vocational Education and Training Authority (VETA), as well as 21 institutions across Tanzania that offer training in 93 lower-skill trades. VETA sets training standards and provides for the registry, assessment, and accreditation of private vocational training institutions and the development of appropriate curricula. VETA training is largely supply driven. The infrequent sector-specific labor market studies do not keep pace with the changing requirements on the demand side. The fields covered in the training include agriculture and food processing, automobile repair and maintenance, electrical engineering, machine operation, textile production, carpentry, masonry, plumbing, road construction, furniture-making, hospitality, and mining. There are also more than 900 private training and vocational education institutions accredited and monitored through the VETA system, which provides indirect support through curriculum development, testing materials, and technical assistance. In 2006, about 80,000 students—1 percent of the labor market—were enrolled in vocational education and training schools, about three-quarters of which were private institutions.

The government established the National Council for Technical Education (NACTE) within the Ministry of Education in 2001. Responsible for regulating technical education in Tanzania, NACTE is also responsible for setting training standards and registering, assessing, accrediting, and coordinating public and private technical education institutions. Unlike the institutions managed through VETA, NACTE is purely a regulatory body; it does not operate schools. Also unlike the VETA institutions, students entering NACTE-certified schools must have completed secondary school. The subjects covered in NACTE technical education facilities include agriculture, natural resources, and the environment; business and management; engineering; health and allied sciences; and planning and welfare. NACTE supports 203 technical education institutions in Tanzania, 100 of which are private.

The following recommendations address the main weaknesses of Tanzania's vocational and technical education system:

• At 6 percent, the skill development levy (payroll tax) is much higher than the international average of 1–3 percent. Private companies obtain little for their share in the levy, which increases their costs and reduces their competitiveness because they must still train their employees. The levy should be lowered, and part of the revenue should be returned to SMEs in the form of training vouchers.

- The existence of two vocational and technical education structures—the VETA and NACTE systems—is inefficient and results in service duplication and waste. Moreover, because VETA is both a regulatory body and a training provider, there is a conflict of interest. Vocational and technical training should be unified into a cohesive framework. The VETA system should be responsible exclusively for skill delivery and the operation of VETA schools. NACTE should act exclusively as a vocational and technical education and training regulatory and accreditation body, and it should work directly with private training providers to ensure quality.

- The VETA and NACTE skill-delivery systems are not responsive to the needs of business and industry. VETA-certified training institutions are supply driven and do not meet the skill requirements of industry. The training is focused on imparting knowledge rather than skills, and graduates are not prepared to meet the demands of the labor market. The VETA and NACTE systems should be urgently reformed on the basis of skill competency. NACTE management should reflect the needs of the private sector to render the skill-delivery system more responsive to changing requirements. Adding an online national jobs board to the Labor Exchange Center of the Ministry of Labor would be useful in identifying the skills in demand, while helping graduates find work.

- The VETA and NACTE systems focus on training in professional and technical skills and neglect entrepreneurial and management skills. To address this issue, use could be made of the Entrepreneurship Development Center of the Faculty of Commerce and Management at the University of Dar es Salaam, which already provides relevant consultancy and training for SMEs. Likewise, the College of Business Education, with campuses in Dar es Salaam, Dodoma, and Mwanza, offers business training that includes entrepreneurship development. SIDO and some nongovernmental organizations have small training programs in business development and management that should be strengthened. Initiatives should also be undertaken to create sectoral institutions in training, advisory services, and business incubation, with technical assistance from the donor community and in collaboration with sectoral associations. The IIDS includes a recommendation that the government help introduce a Kaizen program—a proven program for managerial training that is used widely in Africa—on a commercial basis among large companies, combined with technical assistance for SMEs through SIDO and sectoral associations (World Bank 2011).

Institutional Support and Coordination

Implementing an industrial strategy for Tanzania will require effective public and private institutions and strong coordination among government agencies, the private sector, and donors. While many institutions will be involved, the Ministry of Industry and Trade, SIDO, sectoral associations, and the Planning Commission will take the lead. The Planning Commission in the Office of the President, together with the Ministry of Industry and Trade, can facilitate the needed coordination through the current Five-Year Plan (2011–15). However, though crucial, institutional support will not be able to solve every issue. So institutions should not supplant the private sector in establishing industries, but should aid in mitigating risk, offer supportive policies, and provide basic infrastructure.

Policy Recommendations

There are several key requirements for the effective implementation of our proposed policy actions:

- *Demonstrating high-level political commitment:* The proposed policy actions contemplate fresh investment by local and foreign investors to expand production and introduce new technology in the four sectors we have identified. Investors need assurances from the highest levels of the government of program continuity and a supportive policy agenda. The creation of a high-level committee in the Tanzania National Business Council to oversee implementation and to have direct access to top government leaders would make the reforms more credible.

- *Ensuring effective policy coordination:* The responsibility for formulating and implementing the proposed reforms would reside with several public and private institutions, each focusing on a different aspect of the reform program. Success requires effective coordination among these institutions, as well as with the private sector and the donor community. The IIDS assigns responsibility for implementation to the Ministry of Industry and Trade and its affiliated agencies. The implementation capacity of the ministry and these affiliated agencies should be strengthened substantially. The Planning Commission, in close cooperation with the Ministry of Industry and Trade, could be responsible for coordination among government agencies, the private sector, and donors in the context of the current Five-Year Plan.

- *Building strong public-private partnerships:* Both the public and private sectors lack sufficient capacity to formulate and implement effective policies. Building strong partnerships is thus necessary to leverage this limited capacity and ensure harmonized and coordinated policies. Implementation capacity is weakest at the district level, where light manufacturing enterprises, particularly micro and small enterprises, need the most help. Effective partnerships among local governments, the local SIDO offices, sectoral associations, and other public and private institutions could help bridge gaps in capacity. Public-private partnerships could be useful in other areas as well, including financing for micro and small enterprises, entrepreneurship, and technical training. Despite the fears of entrepreneurs at the prospect of upgrading skills among employees who may then leave for better jobs, supporting training programs that target specific industrial clusters through cluster associations or other independent entities in individual industrial clusters is an effective way to generate tangible results given the similarity of skill requirements, the labor-pooling effect, and the knowledge flows within clusters.

- *Coordinating donor assistance:* Substantial donor assistance will be needed to implement the proposed program, particularly in building capacity in public and private institutions, assisting agencies in their support for SMEs, establishing vocational training and business incubation facilities, and strengthening business associations. There are already many donor programs in these areas, including programs funded by the European Union (EU), the Japan International Cooperation Agency, the Nordic countries, the U.K. Department for International Development, the United Nations Conference on Trade and Development, the United Nations Industrial Development Organization, and the U.S. Agency for International Development. The impact has been limited because of the small size of some of these programs and the lack of local capacity to sustain the programs once donor support ends. Government coordination of donor programs is needed to avoid overlaps, merge smaller programs for greater impact, and ensure that the programs are demand driven and cover components of the light manufacturing program.

- *Addressing governance and political economy issues:* The recommended policy package includes both market-based policies and selective government interventions. To avoid serious governance missteps, two principles should guide actions:
  - Government interventions should aim not at protecting individual companies, but at improving the policy environment for all firms in the sectors selected; unsuccessful companies must be allowed to fail.
  - A key objective of the interventions should be to foster competition (for example, by reducing entry costs and risks) and to address issues of coordination and externalities (Lin 2012).

Notes

1. The government abandoned the fourth Five-Year Plan in 1980. Thereafter, the development agenda was fixed primarily through programs prepared by ministries or agencies focusing on specific sectors. While these programs have been prepared on the basis of national strategies such as the IIDS, implementation has not been well coordinated. The reintroduction of five-year plans, under the responsibility of the Planning Commission, is expected to help in coordinating implementation and monitoring.

2. For an example and more details, see "Quality Service, with Better Service Always," Pride Tanzania Ltd, Arusha, Tanzania, http://pride-tz.org.

3. FinMark Trust, the Steadman Group, and the National Bureau of Statistics conducted two financial surveys related to this program, FinScope I in 2006 and FinScope II in 2009. For details, see the website of the Financial Sector Deepening Trust, at http://www.fsdt.or.tz.

4. For details, see the website of the Financial Sector Deepening Trust, at http://www.fsdt.or.tz.

5. As reported in business surveys in Tanzania conducted by FinScope. See "Tanzania," FinScope, Johannesburg, http://www.finscope.co.za/tanzania.html.

6. To some extent, the overtaxation of labor also helps explain the decision of many firms and many workers to remain in the informal sector.

7. For more details on these steps, see "Association of Tanzania Employers (ATE): Skills Development Assessment," JE Austin Associates, Arlington, VA, http://best-ac.org/wp-content/uploads/ATE-2011-05-Skills-Development-Assessment-JE-Austin.pdf.

References

Fafchamps, Marcel, and Simon Quinn. 2012. "Results of Sample Surveys of Firms." In *Performance of Manufacturing Firms in Africa: An Empirical Analysis*, edited by Hinh T. Dinh and George R. G. Clarke, 139–211. Washington, DC: World Bank.

Lin, Justin Yifu. 2012. *New Structural Economics: A Framework for Rethinking Development and Policy*. Washington, DC: World Bank.

MIT (Tanzania, Ministry of Industry and Trade). 2011a. *Integrated Industrial Development Strategy 2025*. MIT, Dar es Salaam, Tanzania.

———. 2011b. "Development Framework and Action Plans for Integrated Industrial Development Strategy 2025." MIT, Dar es Salaam, Tanzania.

MOF (Tanzania, Ministry of Finance and Economic Affairs). 2000. *National Microfinance Policy*. May, Government Printer, Dar es Salaam, Tanzania. http://www.tanzania.go.tz/pdf/nationalmicrofinancepolicy.pdf.

World Bank. 2011. *Kaizen for Managerial Skills Improvement in Small and Medium Enterprises: An Impact Evaluation Study*. Vol. 4 of *Light Manufacturing in Africa: Targeted Policies to Enhance Private Investment and Create Jobs*. Washington, DC: World Bank. http://go.worldbank.org/4Y1QF5FIB0.

A Matrix of Recommended Policy Actions to Accelerate Light Industry Development

The main findings of our study on Tanzania, including the key constraints and the policy actions needed to overcome them, are summarized in the following action matrix. The matrix contains a large number of measures required to bring about the much-needed structural transformation of the Tanzanian economy for significant, sustained growth in light manufacturing. It provides a reference point and defines a medium- to long-term roadmap to full transformation that can lift workers to higher productivity and more well paying jobs. The matrix is tentative. Some of the proposed measures require further discussion with stakeholders before they can become concrete policy actions.

Table A.1 Recommended Policy Actions to Accelerate the Development of Light Manufacturing, Tanzania

Policy area	Short-term actions	Medium-term actions	Long-term actions
Export incentives and trade logistics	Phase out nontariff barriers in collaboration with the East African Community and foster partnership with the private sector in monitoring such barriers.	Same as short term	
	Restructure the duty drawback system to expedite the reimbursement of import duties to exporters.	Same as short term	

table continues next page

Table A.1 Recommended Policy Actions to Accelerate the Development of Light Manufacturing, Tanzania (continued)

Policy area	Short-term actions	Medium-term actions	Long-term actions
	Establish one-stop border posts in collaboration with the governments of neighboring countries (both East African Community and Southern African Development Community neighbors) and proactively push for early adoption of East African Community guidelines on one-stop border posts by the East African Legislative Assembly. Reduce the number of official police checkpoints and monitor and control the existence of unofficial checkpoints; promote the co-location of checkpoints by the police and by other agencies such as the Tanzania Revenue Authority and the Tanzania National Roads Agency. Establish the single-window system, the Port Community System, at Dar es Salaam Port.		
Labor absenteeism	Experiment in pilot studies with variations on the piece-based wage system; identify the causes and take corrective measures.	Scale up the results of the pilot studies if successful	Same as medium term
		Facilitate affordable housing in areas of business concentration and set up industrial parks and sectoral clusters with residential facilities.	Same as medium term
	Gradually reduce the skill development levy from 6 percent to 1–3 percent (the global average) and allocate part of the revenue to small and medium businesses as training vouchers.	Same as short term	Same as short term
Industrial parks and sector clusters	Assess the performance of the current system of special economic zones (SEZs) and export processing zones (EPZs).	Continue to review fiscal incentives	

table continues next page

Table A.1 Recommended Policy Actions to Accelerate the Development of Light Manufacturing, Tanzania (continued)

Policy area	Short-term actions	Medium-term actions	Long-term actions
	Build the staff capacity of the Export Processing Zones Authority (EPZA) in handling public-private partnership projects.		
	Clarify the role of the EPZA with respect to the Tanzania Investment Center in facilitating investor services in the SEZs.		
	Rationalize the current fiscal incentives provided to investors located in zones and introduce more performance-based incentives.		
	Develop common standards (assessment criteria) for infrastructure service quality within zones.		
		Give the EPZA adequate autonomy. Ensure at least 50 percent representation of the private sector on the EPZA board.	
		Place the EPZA under a central entity (Office of the President, Office of the Prime Minister, or the Ministry of Finance). Locate the EPZA and the Tanzania Investment Center under the same ministry. Establish the budgetary autonomy of the EPZA.	
	Develop a pilot cluster for small businesses in one of the four sectors under examination, in collaboration with local governments, the EPZA, and sectoral associations.		
Electric power supply	Revise the Electricity Act to encourage private investment in power utilities.		
	Waive the import taxes on the equipment used in the generation, transmission, and distribution of electricity.	Accelerate the implementation of power utility projects.	

table continues next page

Table A.1 Recommended Policy Actions to Accelerate the Development of Light Manufacturing, Tanzania *(continued)*

Policy area	Short-term actions	Medium-term actions	Long-term actions
Apparel	Encourage companies to reduce labor absenteeism by experimenting with different piece-based wage systems.	Increase competition in trucking by opening it to new entrants, including foreign companies, and creating a level playing field for domestic companies.	Improve port operations. To lower logistics and transport costs and reduce delays, rehabilitate the railroad lines from Dar es Salaam to Mwanza.
	Lower the fuel tax and import tariffs on trucks and spare parts to reduce the free-on-board (f.o.b.) production cost for manufactured goods by about 0.5 percent.	Encourage investment in the spinning and weaving industries to reduce import dependence. Because these industries are capital-, technology-, and skill-intensive, attracting foreign direct investment (FDI) (preferably in partnership with local capital) and strengthening skills training are essential for making these segments of the value chain competitive.	
	Eliminate all import tariffs on apparel inputs (now 10–35 percent) to enable exporters to resell their material waste, thereby reducing production costs by 1 percent; facilitate links between large exporters and small, domestic producers; and enable implementation of a green customs channel for apparel, an inexpensive reform.		
	Set up plug-and-play industrial parks in areas with input-sourcing potential (in addition to the Bagamoyo master planning process) to provide space for apparel and garment manufacturers.		
Leather and leather products	Gradually lower and eventually remove the export tax on raw hides and skins.	Same as short term	Same as short term

table continues next page

Table A.1 Recommended Policy Actions to Accelerate the Development of Light Manufacturing, Tanzania (continued)

Policy area	Short-term actions	Medium-term actions	Long-term actions
	Strengthen the advocacy and technical assistance roles of sectoral associations.	Same as short term	Commercialize the livestock sector by encouraging ranch-leasing and creating leather sector clusters in appropriate locations.
	Encourage new investment in tanning and leather products, essential for renewing the leather industry. FDI, preferably in partnership with local companies, should be encouraged, and industrial clusters should be formed. Set up training in entrepreneurship, management, technical, and design skills.	Same as short term	Same as short term
	Enhance extension services, particularly in crossbreeding, disease control, slaughter training, preservation practices, quality improvement, and the potential value of hides and skins. These measures will need donor support to be implemented successfully and expeditiously.	Same as short term	Same as short term
	Revise the 1963 Hides and Skins Trade Act to include a grading and market information system on prices so that farmers can receive fair pay for good-quality hides and skins.	Same as short term	Same as short term
	Strengthen enforcement mechanisms to implement effective regulations related to slaughtering, preserving, and transporting livestock. Recruit, train, and employ independent inspectors and graders at collection centers.	Strengthen policy coordination and institutional capacity in both the public and private sectors. One option is to establish a Leather Board (similar to the Cotton Board) as a regulatory and policy-coordination body managed jointly by all stakeholders.	
Wood and wood products	Improve worker skills through formal and informal training (Kaizen method).	Same as short term	Improve incentives to encourage investment in plantation forestry.

table continues next page

Table A.1 **Recommended Policy Actions to Accelerate the Development of Light Manufacturing, Tanzania** *(continued)*

Policy area	Short-term actions	Medium-term actions	Long-term actions
	Encourage new investment and technology upgrades through FDI (preferably as joint ventures), training for technical and modern design skills, and the establishment of integrated wood products clusters close to the source materials.	Same as short term Strengthen institutions and policy coordination by establishing a Wood Products Board (similar to the Cotton Board) as a regulatory and policy-coordination body managed jointly by all stakeholders to ensure the coordination and promotion of the entire value chain.	Same as short and medium terms
Agroprocessing	Establish commercial farming in planned corridors. This initiative will require strong public-private partnerships to build the necessary infrastructure and arrange services, such as farm machinery and equipment leasing.	Set up agroprocessing clusters as part of SEZs to encourage the processing industry.	Same as short and medium terms
	Encourage contract farming to improve the access of small farmers to agricultural inputs and services and to formalize the connections between smallholders and the agroprocessing industry. Implement this arrangement as a pilot initiative and encourage wider adoption if the pilot initiative is successful.	Same as short term	Same as short term
	Establish industrial clusters as a pilot initiative	Accelerate cluster formation through collaboration among the main stakeholders (such as local governments, the EPZA, and sectoral associations) in building the necessary infrastructure, establishing supply chain management, creating training-with-production services, and developing market links.	Same as medium term

table continues next page

Table A.1 Recommended Policy Actions to Accelerate the Development of Light Manufacturing, Tanzania *(continued)*

Policy area	Short-term actions	Medium-term actions	Long-term actions
	Enhance training services for the production of food under hygienic conditions. Scale up successful initiatives, such as the planned establishment of food processing training and production centers at the Small Industries Development Organization (SIDO), to be financed by the Korea International Cooperation Agency.	To strengthen the regulatory framework and improve standards, certification, and control management in agroprocessing, restructure the Tanzania Bureau of Standards and the Tanzania Food and Drug Authority and equip them with modern technology and skills.	Same as medium term
		Once the feasibility study has been completed, the government should seek FDI in the sector, preferably in partnership with local entrepreneurs.	Same as medium term
	Encourage the packaging industry by providing technical assistance to the agroprocessing sector. Conduct a feasibility study on investment in the production of packaging material.	Strengthen sectoral associations such as the Tanzania Agricultural Council so that they can coordinate policy. To be effective in this role, the council should be represented in private umbrella institutions, such as the Tanzania National Business Council and the Tanzania Private Sector Foundation.	Same as short and medium terms
Institutional issues	Unify the vocational and technical education systems. In this unified system, the Vocational Education and Training Authority (VETA) would be exclusively responsible for skill delivery and for operating its vocational education schools. The National Council for Technical Education (NACTE) would become the sole regulatory and accreditation body for vocational education and technical training, working with private training providers to ensure quality.	Same as short term	Same as short term

table continues next page

Table A.1 Recommended Policy Actions to Accelerate the Development of Light Manufacturing, Tanzania *(continued)*

Policy area	Short-term actions	Medium-term actions	Long-term actions
	Accelerate the implementation of a competence-based education and training system under the guidance of the vocational education and technical training institutions and improve the effectiveness of this system.	Same as short term	Same as short term
	Restructure the management of the National Council for Technical Education so that a majority of the members represent the private sector.	Same as short term	Same as short term
	Strengthen the Labor Exchange Center of the Ministry of Labor through an online national jobs board to help identify the skills that are in demand and to help graduates find work. Support cluster-targeting skill development programs, in partnership with business associations and cluster associations.	Same as short term	Same as short term

The Institutional Support Structure and Value Chain, Four Sectors

Figure B.1 The Cotton-to-Garment Market and Institutional Support Structure, Tanzania

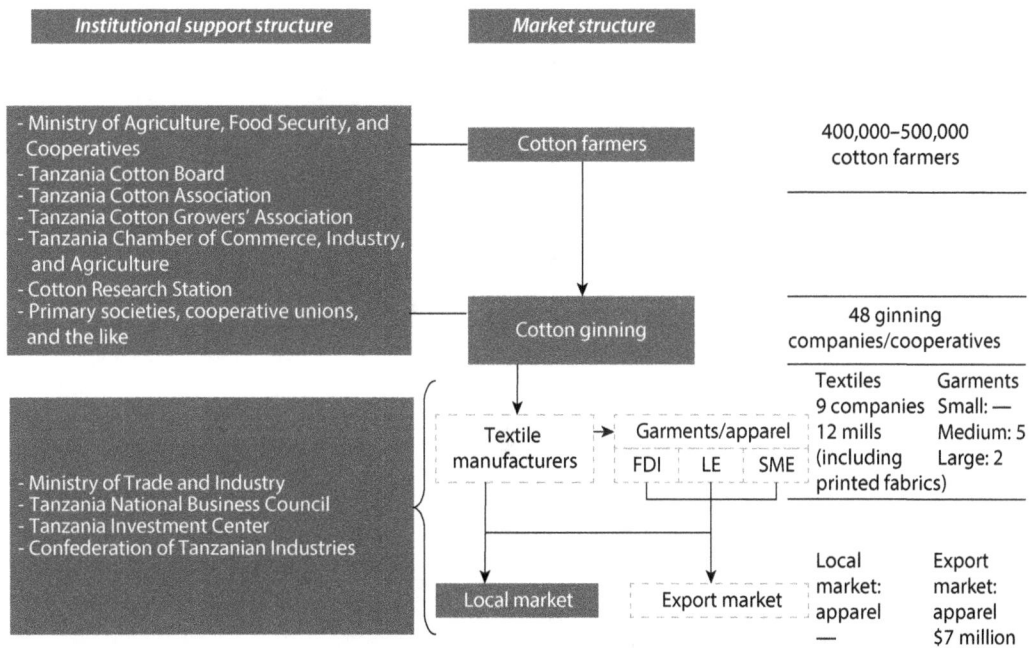

Source: GDS 2011.
Note: Dashed lines indicate a weak link, lack of organization, and areas where technical support is needed to strengthen links along the supply chain. The number of farmers and the number of ginning, textile, and garment companies represent the situation in 2008. — = not available; FDI = foreign-invested enterprises; LE = large enterprises; SME = small and medium enterprises.

Figure B.2 The Polo Shirt Value Chain, Tanzania

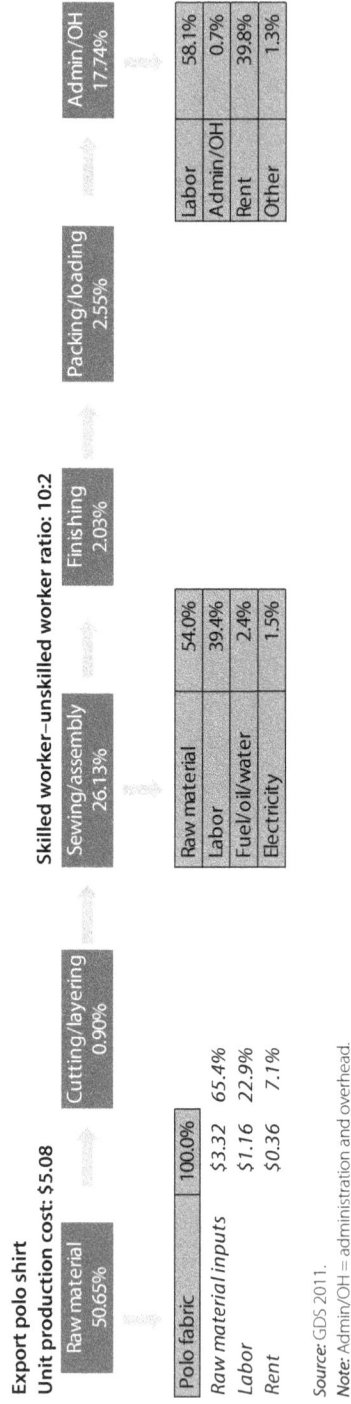

Export polo shirt
Unit production cost: $5.08

Raw material 50.65%	Cutting/layering 0.90%

Polo fabric	100.0%
Raw material inputs	*$3.32*	*65.4%*
Labor	*$1.16*	*22.9%*
Rent	*$0.36*	*7.1%*

Skilled worker–unskilled worker ratio: 10:2

Sewing/assembly 26.13%	Finishing 2.03%	Packing/loading 2.55%	Admin/OH 17.74%

Raw material	54.0%
Labor	39.4%
Fuel/oil/water	2.4%
Electricity	1.5%

Labor	58.1%
Admin/OH	0.7%
Rent	39.8%
Other	1.3%

Source: GDS 2011.
Note: Admin/OH = administration and overhead.

Figure B.3 The Polo Shirt Value Chain, Guangdong, China

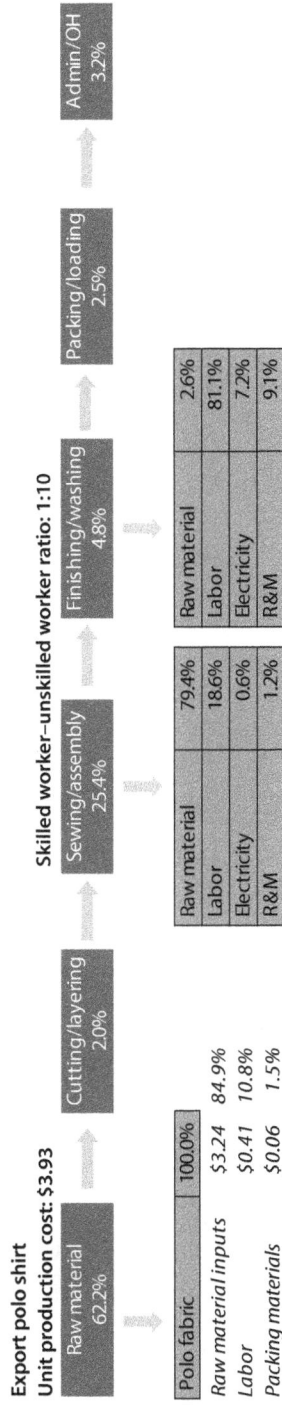

Export polo shirt
Unit production cost: $3.93

Skilled worker–unskilled worker ratio: 1:10

| Raw material 62.2% | → | Cutting/layering 2.0% | → | Sewing/assembly 25.4% | → | Finishing/washing 4.8% | → | Packing/loading 2.5% | → | Admin/OH 3.2% |

Polo fabric	100.0%
Raw material inputs	*$3.24*	*84.9%*
Labor	*$0.41*	*10.8%*
Packing materials	*$0.06*	*1.5%*

Sewing/assembly	
Raw material	79.4%
Labor	18.6%
Electricity	0.6%
R&M	1.2%

Finishing/washing	
Raw material	2.6%
Labor	81.1%
Electricity	7.2%
R&M	9.1%

Source: GDS 2011.
Note: Admin/OH = administration and overhead; R&M = repairs and maintenance.

Figure B.4 The Footwear Market and Institutional Support Structure, Tanzania

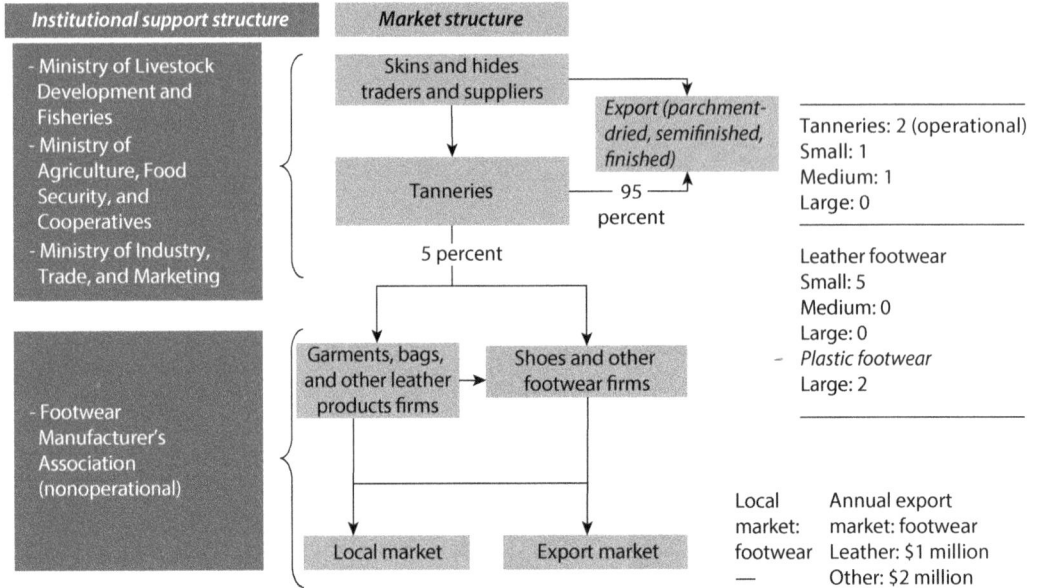

Institutional support structure	Market structure

- Ministry of Livestock Development and Fisheries
- Ministry of Agriculture, Food Security, and Cooperatives
- Ministry of Industry, Trade, and Marketing

- Footwear Manufacturer's Association (nonoperational)

Skins and hides traders and suppliers

Export (parchment-dried, semifinished, finished)

Tanneries — 95 — percent

5 percent

Garments, bags, and other leather products firms → Shoes and other footwear firms

Local market   Export market

Tanneries: 2 (operational)
Small: 1
Medium: 1
Large: 0

Leather footwear
Small: 5
Medium: 0
Large: 0
- Plastic footwear
Large: 2

Local market: footwear —

Annual export market: footwear
Leather: $1 million
Other: $2 million

Source: GDS 2011.
Note: — = not available.

Figure B.5 The Leather Loafer Value Chain, Tanzania

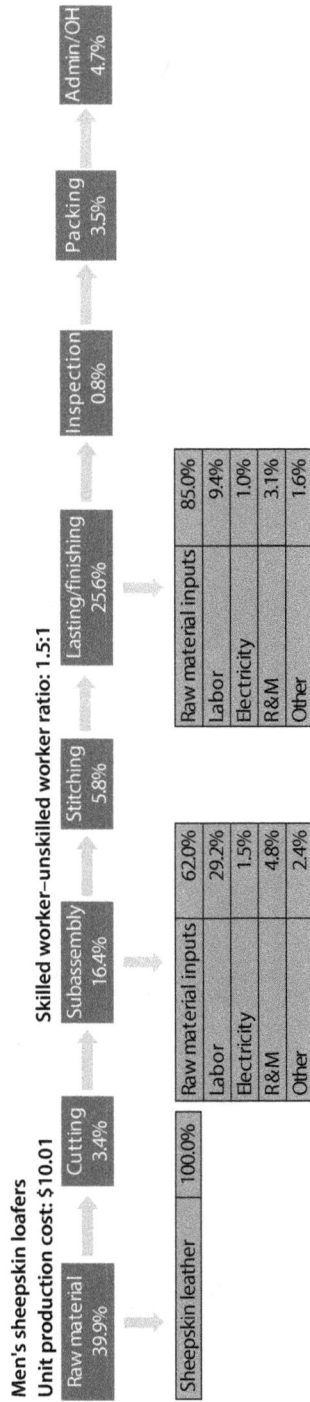

Men's sheepskin loafers

Unit production cost: $10.01   **Skilled worker–unskilled worker ratio: 1.5:1**

| Raw material 39.9% | → | Cutting 3.4% | → | Subassembly 16.4% | → | Stitching 5.8% | → | Lasting/finishing 25.6% | → | Inspection 0.8% | → | Packing 3.5% | → | Admin/OH 4.7% |

| Sheepskin leather | 100.0% |

Raw material inputs	62.0%
Labor	29.2%
Electricity	1.5%
R&M	4.8%
Other	2.4%

Raw material inputs	85.0%
Labor	9.4%
Electricity	1.0%
R&M	3.1%
Other	1.6%

Source: GDS 2011.

Note: Admin/OH = administration and overhead; R&M = repairs and maintenance.

Figure B.6 The Leather Loafer Value Chain, Guangdong, China

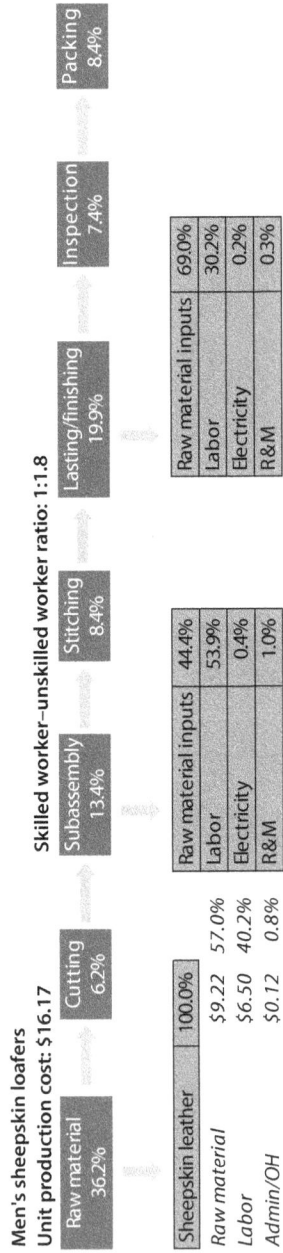

Men's sheepskin loafers
Unit production cost: $16.17

Skilled worker–unskilled worker ratio: 1:1.8

| Raw material 36.2% | Cutting 6.2% | Subassembly 13.4% | Stitching 8.4% | Lasting/finishing 19.9% | Inspection 7.4% | Packing 8.4% |

Sheepskin leather	100.0%
Raw material	$9.22	57.0%
Labor	$6.50	40.2%
Admin/OH	$0.12	0.8%

Raw material inputs	44.4%
Labor	53.9%
Electricity	0.4%
R&M	1.0%

Raw material inputs	69.0%
Labor	30.2%
Electricity	0.2%
R&M	0.3%

Source: GDS 2011.

Note: Admin/OH = administration and overhead; R&M = repairs and maintenance.

Figure B.7 Wood and Wood Products Market and Institutional Support Structure, Tanzania

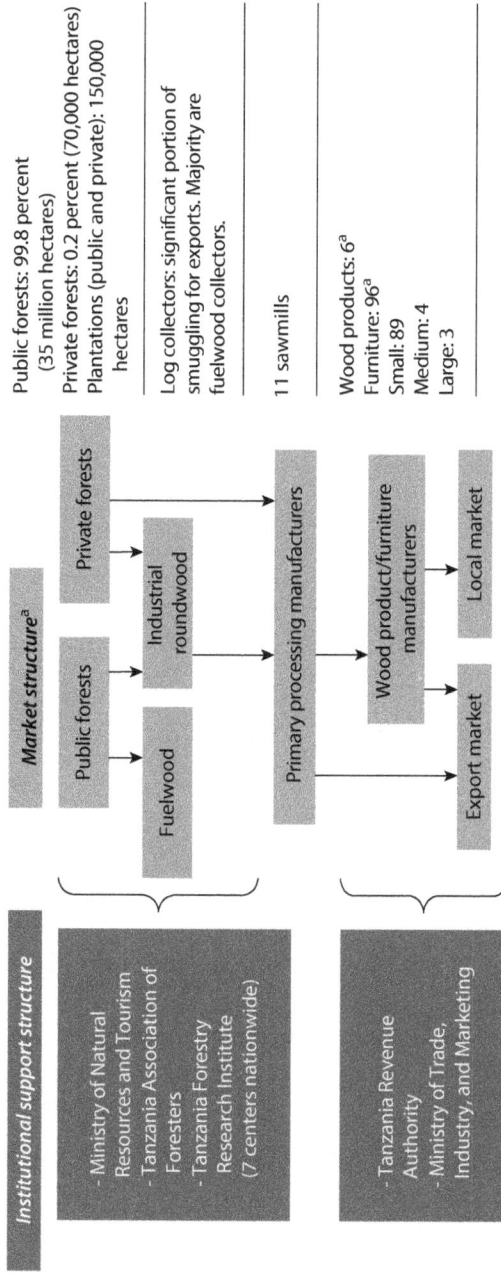

Market structure[a]	
Public forests	Private forests
Fuelwood	Industrial roundwood

Primary processing manufacturers

Wood product/furniture manufacturers

Export market — Local market

Institutional support structure

- Ministry of Natural Resources and Tourism
- Tanzania Association of Foresters
- Tanzania Forestry Research Institute (7 centers nationwide)

- Tanzania Revenue Authority
- Ministry of Trade, Industry, and Marketing

Public forests: 99.8 percent (35 million hectares)
Private forests: 0.2 percent (70,000 hectares)
Plantations (public and private): 150,000 hectares

Log collectors: significant portion of smuggling for exports. Majority are fuelwood collectors.

11 sawmills

Wood products: 6[a]
Furniture: 96[a]
Small: 89
Medium: 4
Large: 3

Source: GDS 2011.
a. Excludes microenterprises, small enterprises, and workshops employing fewer than 10 people.

Figure B.8 The Wooden Chair Value Chain, Tanzania

Local market wooden chair, unupholstered
Unit production cost: $33.42

Lumber price ($/m³): $275

Skilled worker–unskilled worker ratio: 2:1

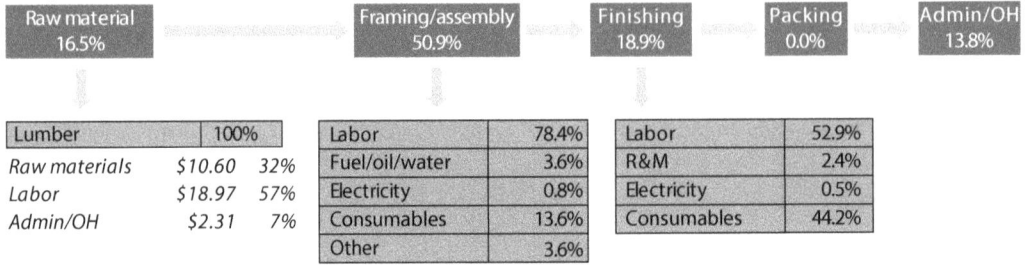

| Raw material 16.5% | Framing/assembly 50.9% | Finishing 18.9% | Packing 0.0% | Admin/OH 13.8% |

Lumber		100%
Raw materials	$10.60	32%
Labor	$18.97	57%
Admin/OH	$2.31	7%

Labor	78.4%
Fuel/oil/water	3.6%
Electricity	0.8%
Consumables	13.6%
Other	3.6%

Labor	52.9%
R&M	2.4%
Electricity	0.5%
Consumables	44.2%

Source: GDS 2011.
Note: Admin/OH = administration and overhead; R&M = repairs and maintenance.

Figure B.9 The Wooden Chair Value Chain, China

Export (and local) wooden chair, unupholstered
Unit production cost: $12.67

Lumber price ($/m³): $369

Skilled worker–unskilled worker ratio: 1:8

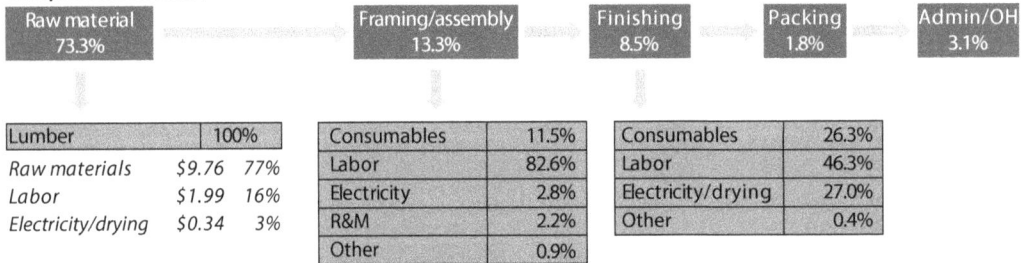

| Raw material 73.3% | Framing/assembly 13.3% | Finishing 8.5% | Packing 1.8% | Admin/OH 3.1% |

Lumber		100%
Raw materials	$9.76	77%
Labor	$1.99	16%
Electricity/drying	$0.34	3%

Consumables	11.5%
Labor	82.6%
Electricity	2.8%
R&M	2.2%
Other	0.9%

Consumables	26.3%
Labor	46.3%
Electricity/drying	27.0%
Other	0.4%

Source: GDS 2011.
Note: Admin/OH = administration and overhead; R&M = repairs and maintenance.

Figure B.10 The Wheat Milling Value Chain, Tanzania

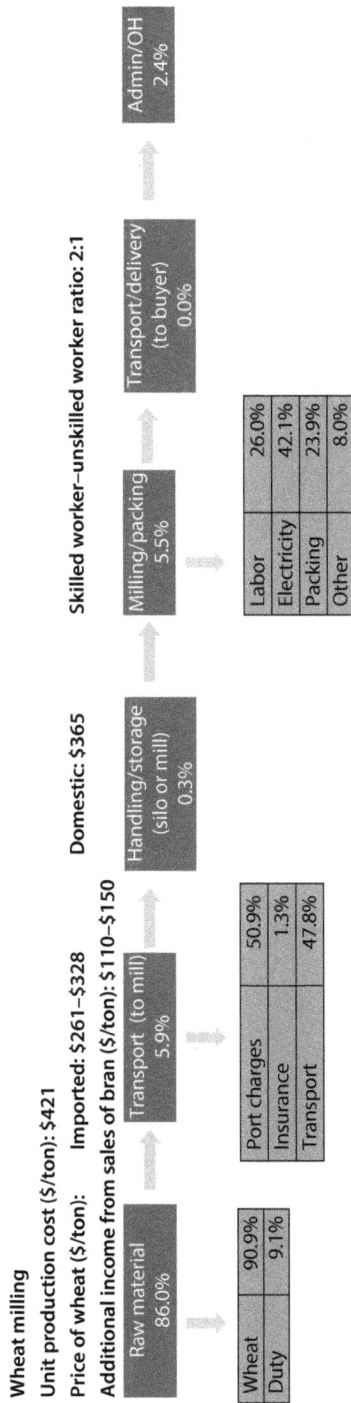

Wheat milling

Unit production cost ($/ton): $421

Price of wheat ($/ton):   Imported: $261–$328   Domestic: $365   Skilled worker–unskilled worker ratio: 2:1

Additional income from sales of bran ($/ton): $110–$150

| Raw material 86.0% | Transport (to mill) 5.9% | Handling/storage (silo or mill) 0.3% | Milling/packing 5.5% | Transport/delivery (to buyer) 0.0% | Admin/OH 2.4% |

| Wheat | 90.9% |
| Duty | 9.1% |

Port charges	50.9%
Insurance	1.3%
Transport	47.8%

Labor	26.0%
Electricity	42.1%
Packing	23.9%
Other	8.0%

Source: GDS 2011.
Note: Admin/OH = administration and overhead.

Reference

GDS (Global Development Solutions). 2011. *The Value Chain and Feasibility Analysis; Domestic Resource Cost Analysis.* Vol. 2 of *Light Manufacturing in Africa: Targeted Policies to Enhance Private Investment and Create Jobs.* Washington, DC: World Bank. http://go.worldbank.org/6G2A3TFI20.

Environmental Benefits Statement

The World Bank is committed to reducing its environmental footprint. In support of this commitment, the Office of the Publisher leverages electronic publishing options and print-on-demand technology, which is located in regional hubs worldwide. Together, these initiatives enable print runs to be lowered and shipping distances decreased, resulting in reduced paper consumption, chemical use, greenhouse gas emissions, and waste.

The Office of the Publisher follows the recommended standards for paper use set by the Green Press Initiative. Whenever possible, books are printed on 50% to 100% postconsumer recycled paper, and at least 50% of the fiber in our book paper is either unbleached or bleached using Totally Chlorine Free (TCF), Processed Chlorine Free (PCF), or Enhanced Elemental Chlorine Free (EECF) processes.

More information about the Bank's environmental philosophy can be found at http://crinfo.worldbank.org/crinfo/environmental_responsibility/index.html.

green press
INITIATIVE

www.ingramcontent.com/pod-product-compliance
Lightning Source LLC
Chambersburg PA
CBHW081645280326
41928CB00069B/3092